GYMNASTICS

IN PERSPECTIVE

PHOTOGRAPHY

EILEEN LANGSLEY

DESIGN

DWIGHT NORMILE

PUBLISHED BY

FÉDÉRATION INTERNATIONALE DE GYMNASTIQUE

FONDÉE EN 1881

OFFICIAL WATCH OF WORLD GYMNASTICS

First published in 2000 by:
Fédération Internationale de
Gymnastique,
Rue des Oeuches 10,
2740 Moutier 1,
Switzerland

ISBN 2-9700110-1-8

Photography: Eileen Langsley
Design: Dwight Normile
FIG Liaison: Sandra Stadelmann
Origination and printing:
Roos SA, Crémines

CONTENTS

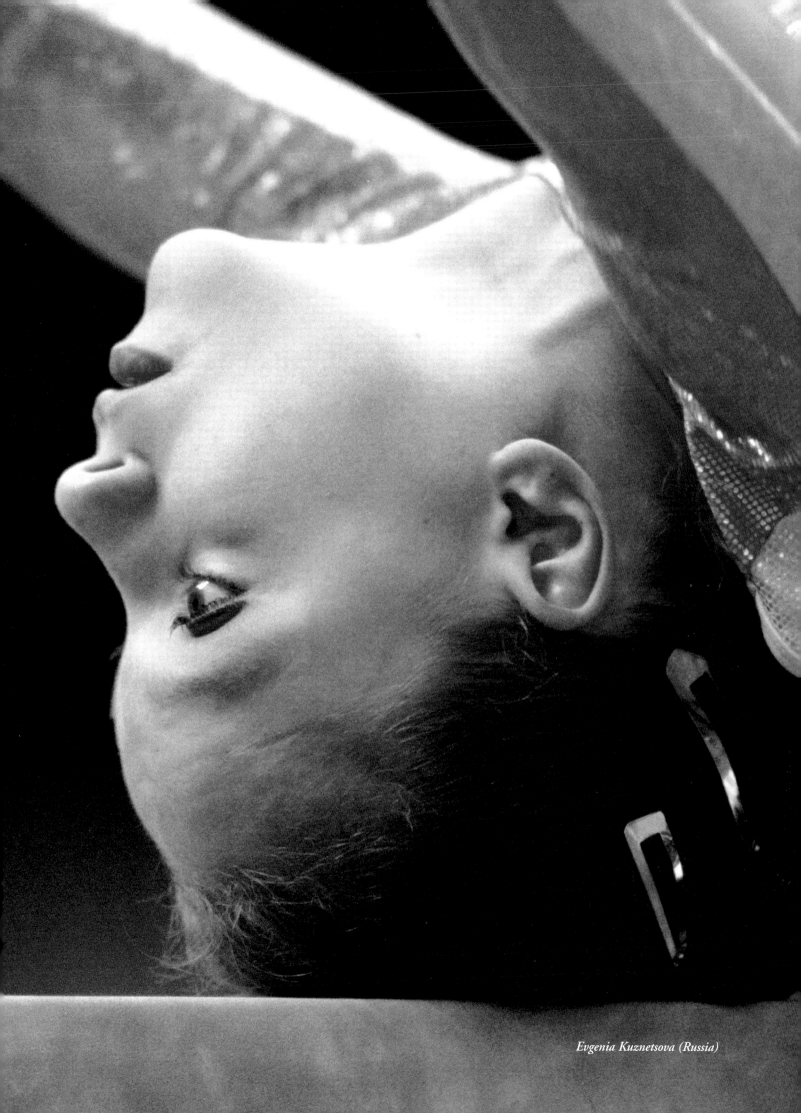

Evgenia Kuznetsova (Russia)

FONDÉE EN 1881

PRESIDENT'S MESSAGE

BY BRUNO GRANDI

T HE FIG herewith presents another collection of photographs taken by the able and expert Eileen Langsley. This new publication underlines the importance that the Executive Committee continues to attach to such initiatives, representing 'stills' of the moments through which gymnastics has passed and being of historical significance in both real and comparative terms. The photos of old indeed take us back to forms of movement and gestures that were then considered superlative, perfect, but cannot stand the test of time if compared with those performed by modern-day champions.

These photographs offer, on the other hand, documentary evidence of the technical and aesthetic evolution of forms and elements produced by man's creativity. And as customs and habits change, so do our views of what is beautiful and perfect. Aesthetic taste is thus dependent on the moment in which we are living, reflecting the vogue of an era. We are aware that 'perfection' has temporal limits too, and that human perfection is also evolving, becoming what we might describe as 'more perfect.'

If we study these pages in greater depth, we might see the cultural-anthropological message that man is writing through aesthetic evolution. An evolution that a greater scientist and student of physics and mathematics such as Professor Zichichi calls 'aesthetic intelligence,' a capacity unique to human beings. Man and man alone has evolved and is continuing to progress in the biological space in which he lives, demonstrating that the frontiers of human knowledge will continue to be pushed back regularly and methodically.

Movement in gymnastics becomes body language, a means of communicating within the permanent relationship between man and his environment. The gymnast is conquering ever-higher peaks in terms of the perfection of his movement in space. In this light, we can see day after day the progress made and the extended frontiers of our sport.

We can no longer conceive of the growth of gymnastics purely in terms of acrobatics or biomechanics, rather of geometric lines upon which the gymnast's performance is built. Unlike all other sports in which sportsmen's records and performances are judged by metric or temporal yardsticks, the continuous evolution of gymnastics is measured by the perfection of the gymnast's movements.

And if after seeing a perfect execution the viewer is moved, it means that the gymnast has not only attained motor perfection but also touched the most genuine and profound sentiments of the spectator.

This is the show we put on—this perhaps our evolution—the forging of an emotional bond through the interpretation given by the gymnast. This is artistic gymnastics. And it is in this light that gymnastics should be viewed and judged within the world sporting movement.

Eileen Langsley has captured these images and 'snapped' the various stages of our sport's history. At the same time she has immortalised the human dramas of the protagonists.

I have often called gymnastics the 'humanism' of sport. Since it encapsulates the anthropological history of man, it is an essential part of motor activity, and it forms a part of aesthetic intelligence, the final stage of man's biological evolution.

Gymnastics knows how to create more unforgettable and moving moments than any other sport due to its kinship to art. It must, therefore, maintain its identity while allowing us to participate in that great adventure of life written down in the mysterious book of our terrestrial existence. ❖

Opposite: The sporting disciplines of the Fédération Internationale de Gymnastique which represent the new era of gymnastics.

Bruno Grandi of Italy is President of the Fédération Internationale de Gymnastique.

LONGINES' CELEBRATION OF GYMNASTICS

I N 1912, when Switzerland's budding amateur athletic associations decided to stage the country's national track and field championships in the city of Basle, Longines was already an 80-year-old company with quite considerable sports timing experience acquired, among other places, at the newly re-established Olympic Games, with timers and chronographs of its own design.

But that year in Basle, Longines had more to offer. Much more. In particular, an astute trip-wire timing system that constituted the first of many significant advances in sport timing—up to today's high-performance MTS 600 system that adds such invaluable speed, flexibility and precision to gymnastics timing and scoring procedures.

All this to say that while Longines' love affair with sport goes back a long time and continues to involve vast expenditures of energy and ingenuity, it has lost none of its passion. As the years passed, Longines timed and helped score all manner of winter and summer competitions. In 1989, the company proudly announced its appointment as official timekeeper of the International Gymnastics Federation (FIG) for all international events in the artistic and rhythmic disciplines, selected Longines watch designs furthermore benefiting from an "Official Watch" status. Over the next few years, the company's teams of engineers and timing experts honed their skills at the international gymnastics competitions held year after year, gradually developing unrivaled expertise in this specialised area.

With ever greater understanding came ever stronger admi-

OFFICIAL WATCH OF WORLD GYMNASTICS

ration for the artistic, athletic and human qualities of gymnasts of both sexes—along with a desire to salute the finest among them with a concrete, tangible memento of their excellence. That memento was to be the Longines Trophy for Elegance (created by the Swiss artist Piero Travaglini) and Longines wristwatch. Established in 1997, it has been regularly awarded ever since, first to female and now also to male athletes.

Unlike purely sport-related distinctions, the Longines Prize for Elegance is awarded on the basis of a broad set of criteria. Nominees are judged according to such "emotional" yardsticks as beauty, charm, charisma and what might be called "innate elegance," in keeping with the personal tastes of an unusual "mixed" jury which, whatever the competition and the venue, includes representatives from the media and the fashion industry along with local and international sport personalities as well as, in every case, Longines president Walter von Känel.

What Longines has given to gymnastics, the sport has returned with interest.

In 1997, the very first Longines Prize for Elegance was awarded at the World Rhythmic Gymnastics Championships, held in Berlin, to Yana Batyrchina of Russia. A year later, that country also provided the second winner, Svetlana Khorkina, at the European Artistic Gymnastics Championships in St. Petersburg. Later that same year in Seville, the Spanish women's team at the World Rhythmic Gymnastics Championships collectively received the Longines Prize for Elegance. It was followed in 1999 by the Hungarian gymnast Viktoria Frater who received the Trophy in Budapest at the European Rhythmic Gymnastics

*Alina Kabaeva (Russia), 1999 world rhythmic champion
and Longines ambassador of Elegance.*

Below: Longines Trophy for Elegance, created in 1997.

Right: The Chinese men's team, 1999 world champions and Longines ambassadors of Elegance.

Opposite: Yana Batyrchina (Russia) first winner of the Longines Prize for Elegance.

Opposite inset top to bottom:

Elena Vitrichenko (Ukraine), voted the most elegant gymnast at the 1999 World Rhythmic Championships in Osaka, Japan.

Prize winner Viktoria Frater (Hungary) at the 1999 European Rhythmic Championships in Budapest, Hungary, with Longines President Walter von Känel and 1996 Olympic champion Ekaterina Serebrianskaya.

Svetlana Khorkina (Russia) and Lu Yufu (China) won the Prize at the 1999 World Artistic Championships in Tianjin, China.

Championships, and Elena Vitrichenko of Ukraine rewarded in Osaka at the World Rhythmic Gymnastics Championships. A few days later, at the World Artistic Gymnastics Championships in the Chinese city of Tianjin, Svetlana Khorkina won her second Longines Prize for Elegance while this distinction was for the first time presented to a male athlete, Chinese gymnast Lu Yufu.

What Longines has given to gymnastics, the sport has returned with interest. The company's close association with this elegant discipline has for instance enabled it to recruit as its ambassadress to rhythmic gymnastics events and circles none other than Alina Kabaeva, a young athlete prodigy who, since 1998, has won such an impressive series of competitions that she is the reigning world champion! Her poise, composure and natural grace make her a perfect representative of the elegance and aesthetic values which Longines holds in high esteem.

Longines is also privileged to count as its collective ambassador the men's artistic gymnastics team of the P.R. of China.

Its impeccable precision and discipline yielded impressive results at the recent World Artistic Gymnastics Championships in Tianjin, China. The crack six-man squad received no less than three gold and two bronze medals—an eminently successful demonstration of the Longines philosophy in action.

With the Longines Prize for Elegance and its choice of ambassadors to world-class competition gymnastics, the company confirms its overriding preoccupation with elegance everywhere—from the world's most prestigious sports arenas to the countless venues of everyday life. "Elegance is an Attitude" affirms Longines' worldwide communication. And more than ever a way of life! ❖

LONGINES®

OFFICIAL WATCH OF WORLD GYMNASTICS

A PERSONAL PERSPECTIVE

BY EILEEN LANGSLEY

FOR those who know me, it's no secret that I consider gymnastics to be the greatest of all sports. A lifetime of involvement has given me a privileged and perhaps unique perspective, first as an enthusiastic if somewhat untalented participant, later as a coach and choreographer, and finally as a member of the gymnastics media, using my camera to capture and preserve some of the sport's most magic moments.

I have been fortunate to have experienced the child's joy of mastering new skills. I have felt the satisfaction of helping young gymnasts to achieve their ambitions and I have been present at some of the most historic moments in the sport. Small wonder that my belief in gymnastics—in all its forms—is so strong.

Whilst the dictionary may dictate that a perspective by defini-

I hope that what my eye has seen, that which has appealed to my spirit and what my camera has recorded, will be significant to others who love the sport and that it invites their personal, subjective response.

tion should be an objective one, there is no doubt that involvement inevitably leads to a subjective point of view as well. As a member of the media I am conscious of my neutral role, on the outside looking in, but I trust that my photography captures the spirit of the sport and provides a meaningful insight to others. I hope that what my eye has seen, that which has appealed to my spirit and what my camera has recorded, will be significant to others who love the sport and that it invites their personal, subjective response.

Gymnastics - In Perspective is published at a momentous time for the FIG, standing as it does on the threshold of a new era. Gymnastics continues to develop apace in all its traditional activities which will now be enhanced by the inclusion of the new disciplines of sports aerobics, trampoline and tumbling, and sports acrobatics, each of which brings a new dimension and its own unique qualities to the world of gymnastics.

My opening statement begs two questions. What makes a sport truly great? What does gymnastics possess that is not present in other sports? All sporting activities have beneficial effects on the physical, mental and social development of their participants and gymnastics is no exception here. The combination of physical excellence with superb artistry can also be matched in other sports, such as figure skating, so what gives me the right to place

gymnastics on a higher pedestal?

The answer to this question came to me at the 1999 Gymnaestrada in Gothenburg, Sweden, when I found myself surrounded by over 22,000 participants, many of whom had taken annual holiday leave to take part in this extraordinary event. Here were people of all ages, nationalities, creeds and races, of all levels of ability and disability, united by the sheer love of gymnastics, a sense of fellowship and the joy of participation. At no other event can the Olympic creed be so apparent: "It is not the winning but the taking part."

General gymnastics is the solid bedrock which is the foundation of the sport. It truly embodies 'Sport for All' and 'Sport for Life,' providing quality of life, health, well-being and physical challenges to countless thousands of people all over the world and from all walks of life. Gymnastics cuts across all social boundaries and cultural backgrounds, uniting those who take part and increasing global understanding through shared experiences. Young people gain personal empowerment, a sense of identity and an excellent grounding in life's greatest values. Which other sport in the world can boast an event such as the Gymnaestrada or claim to provide meaningful activity for people who take part for the sheer fun of it as well as those greatly talented ones who wish to pursue the sport as far as their talents will take them?

Gymnastics has provided some of the most exciting, historic and memorable moments of the Olympic Games and given pleasure and inspiration to millions of viewers all over the world. The Gymnaestrada, too, with its Olympian scale and ethos, has

*Opposite: **Esther Dominguez (Spain)***
*Above left: **Elvire Teza (France)***
*Above: **Krasimir Dunev (Bulgaria)***

enhanced the lives of all who take part.

Gymnastics - In Perspective features the written thoughts of many significant people within the sport of gymnastics, from all over the world. My special thanks go to them for contributing their perspectives. Whilst their writings express a variety of thoughts, views and feelings, what is significant is that they are all united by a common passion for the sport and a belief in its value. There is a belief, too, in the worldwide family that is gymnastics and I trust that this book will be a tribute to all its members.

The millennium ushers in a new era for gymnastics in which new standards of excellence will be forged, matched by grace, artistry and a deceptively apparent ease of execution. There is no limit in the pursuit of excellence and artistry. If a sport can be said to be a reflection of society, then gymnastics truly shows the world at its best and I am privileged to be part of it.   ❖

Eileen Langsley of Great Britain has been the official photographer for the Fédération Internationale de Gymnastique since 1984.

Atlant

A WAY OF LIFE

*Gymnasts' thoughts,
views, perspectives*

A WAY OF LIFE

BY SHANNON MILLER

HILE gymnastics may be an amazing sport to watch, there is something even more extraordinary about the sport itself. It gets in your blood, becomes an integral part of your life. Maybe it's that feeling you get when you learn a new skill, when you feel yourself defying gravity or the confidence you exude when you stick a landing solidly. Or perhaps it's the breathtaking feeling you get when you hit a perfect routine in competition and the crowd goes wild. You know your feet hit the floor and yet … you're still soaring. Then again, it might be the joy of meeting so many people and making friends all over the country—even the world—or the phenomenal sights you get to see. Your involvement in the sport of gymnastics directly or indirectly contributed to these extraordinary experiences!

Then there are the challenges! There have been many throughout my career. Some physical, some mental and some emotional. Gymnastics requires strength in all of these areas, and in turn, this sport makes you even stronger. It didn't take long for me to learn that while gymnastics is certainly physical, it is just as demanding mentally and emotionally. The lessons learned in gymnastics go far beyond how to exercise or to execute a skill. Most importantly, gymnastics was to me a sport of life. It taught me the skills I could use in school, in business, in daily living: how to be patient (skills aren't always learned in a day); how to listen carefully and to follow directions (your safety could depend on listening to your coach); how to be flexible in mind as well as body (sometimes there are last-minute changes in equipment or your routine); how to adapt to the situation (what if a bar grip breaks or the arena floods, as it did at the 1995 Pan American Games?); how to control fear (don't be overwhelmed, you're not alone); how to learn from mistakes and at the same time relegate them to history and move forward. The list could go

In gymnastics, I have learned how to learn. Each day, sometimes each minute, brings something new.

on and on. When you are rotating in the air, that's not a time to waffle; in a split second you have to remember your coaches' directions, implement them, adapt to any changes in the landing surface, observe what's going on around you (even if you are upside down) and control any fear that might be trying to creep in. The same skills you need when the teacher calls on you in class or your boss calls an impromptu meeting and asks you to suggest a solution to an impending problem.

In gymnastics, I have learned how to learn. Each day, and sometimes each minute, brings something new. Those things that frighten you initially can turn out to benefit you. A few butterflies in the stomach just before a competition can stimulate the adrenaline you need to execute a new skill and remind you how exciting it is to compete. Mistakes can teach you to be so much better the next time. Last-minute changes in your competitive routine teach you to literally think on your feet.

I've certainly experienced ups and downs during my gymnastics career. Falling three times off beam in event finals at world championships was definitely a low point. But I survived. Life went on and so did gymnastics. I couldn't change that event but I could learn from it, figure out technically what I did wrong, but more importantly move forward emotionally and mentally. Look inside myself and find real strength. I still loved gymnastics, my coaches and parents hadn't given up on me, there were more meets in which to compete and God was still standing by me.

While there have been a few low points, the wonderful times dominate my memory so much more. Some of the best times of my career occurred at the '92 and '96 Olympics. In 1992, I

Opposite: Shannon Miller (USA)

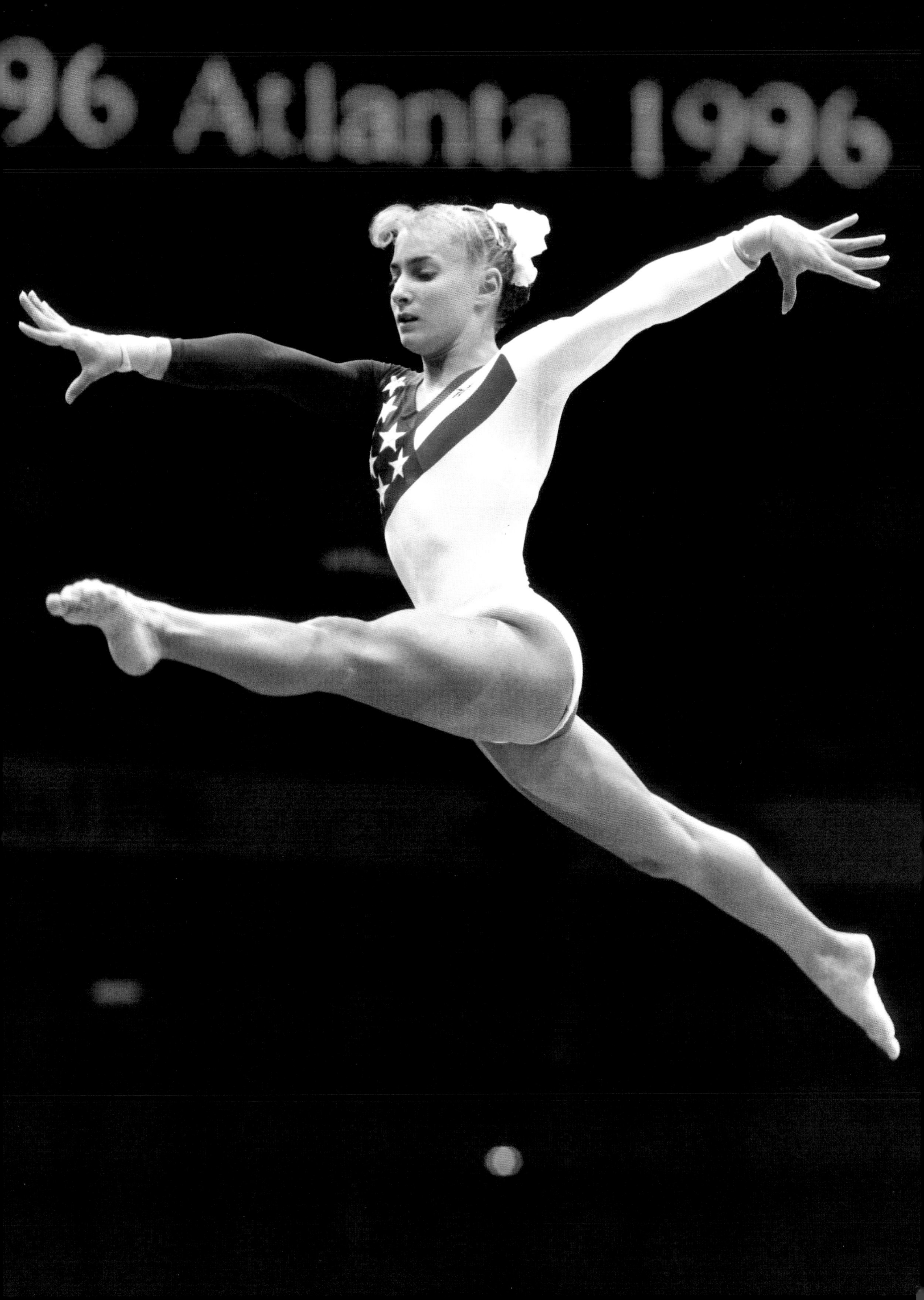
96 Atlanta 1996

approached the Games full of excitement and wonder. I was only 15 and oblivious to much of what was going on around me. My focus was really just doing my gymnastics. I knew very little of what the media were saying, rarely heard any news and really didn't care to hear any. I had a dream and I was living that dream. Following the all-around competition, a reporter asked me if I was sad that I had not won gold. I stared at her in total surprise, almost speechless. My gosh, I had *won* an individual silver Olympic medal. How could I be anything but ecstatic? In 1996 I was older, 19, and the Games were in the United States. Daily, you could feel the energy the Games were generating. You could hardly miss what was going on. The team was charged. We were a diverse group which only added to our strength and success. The pressure seemed more intense during these Games, maybe because I was older, or maybe because I knew more about what was going on and there was the constant onslaught of publicity about the Games, or more likely, it was a combination of all these things. Regardless, the '96 Olympics was every bit as exciting and

---

You cannot imagine the feeling you get when all your hard work materialises in a great routine.

---

awesome as 1992 had been. When the national anthem was played and each team member lovingly clutched her gold medal, there was no doubt what the sport of gymnastics meant to each one of us, why we loved every minute we had spent in the gym and on the competition floor.

There are so many fantastic memories from my gymnastics career. It's hard to choose only a few. I may have wobbled and fallen in the past, but in 1996 the beam felt firm under my feet. Had I not won a medal that day, I would still have felt terrific. You cannot imagine the feeling you get when all your hard work materialises in a great routine, when you execute the skills the way you have imagined yourself doing so many times in your dreams. But many of my wonderful memories come not from a medal or a particular meet. Each time you hear your name chanted by a group of young fans, see the pleased smile of your coaches, hear the cheers of the audience as you land your dismount, get asked by a shy child or a loving grandmother for your autograph, feel the pride of your teammates, or curl up at night with a pleasurably tired body, you've created an incredible memory that really cannot be compared to any of the others. It may be the big meets you consciously remember, but who you really are, are all those

Opposite & Above: **Shannon Miller (USA)**

delightful experiences, all those priceless memories.

I was so fortunate to receive outstanding coaching while still being able to live at home with my family and attend public school. My greatest hope is that I can communicate to the public that the sport of gymnastics can be so beneficial to children of all ages. My family stayed together, I received a good education, I maintained a healthy body and a positive outlook while training and competing at a high level. The advice I give to parents, children and coaches is basically what my parents and coaches have taught me over the years. Set goals, be prepared to work hard to achieve them but never think you have to accomplish all this on your own. There are parents and coaches for support, and more importantly, God is always nearby. He will direct my path and yours as long as we have the courage to follow His lead.

Early in my life I discovered the benefits of setting long-term and short-term goals. You might find it beneficial to have a goal for every week or maybe every day. Something to keep you motivated. However, when setting goals, never fall into the trap of limiting yourself. Just because it hasn't been done doesn't mean you can't do it! It is so easy to make the mistake of restricting ourselves. Bad day—blame it on the coach, too little sleep, too much homework, whatever. But making excuses is a subtle way of limiting ourselves. If you think the coach was asking too much of

you, ask yourself why he demanded you try a certain skill, or why he had you repeat it so many times. Maybe he believes in you and what you are capable of, maybe he wants more for you. Don't make excuses. Look for solutions and you will soon find there are *no limits*! Twenty years ago who would have thought gymnasts would be doing the skills they are now? What tremendous progress. You can be part of this progress if you let yourself. In 1995, when I was 18, the media and general public were of the opinion that I was getting over the hill, a little too old for the big skills; my body couldn't handle the workouts, etc. At 23 I'm still going strong. I love gymnastics and refuse to let anyone put limits on me. When the going gets tough … I remember: With God, all things are possible.

I have tried to apply all the wonderful lessons I've learned through gymnastics to the rest of my life. There is so much I still want to do, so much I haven't yet experienced, things I don't even know about. With no limits, there's no telling what I might yet do. But whatever I do and wherever I go, I plan always to stay in some way involved with the sport of gymnastics. It's in my blood, part of my life! ❖

Shannon Miller of the U.S. won all-around world titles in 1993 and '94 and two golds at the 1996 Olympics (team and balance beam).

WHAT IT ALL MEANS

BY IVAN IVANKOV

WHEN you're born you never know what you want to do or what you want to be in the future. When I started to do gymnastics I never thought about my career and it was just for fun. I just enjoyed it. My parents never thought the sport would become serious. They thought I would have to study and get an education, and if possible, a good education.

But my life took a different turn. Time went on and gymnastics took over my life. Every year it became harder to leave gymnastics. There were good times and bad times, but I think there is one reason to be in gymnastics. It's hard work, but when you finally achieve what you're striving for, it's beautiful and you're

> *It's hard work, but when you finally achieve what you're striving for, it's beautiful and you're very happy.*

very happy. Right now I understand that gymnastics is not my whole life, but it's almost half of my life. And it's a very interesting and unusual life.

In training, sometimes, every day is the same. … If you don't have any goals or any dreams it will be very hard and you can't do it. I think, definitely, you can't do it, because it's really hard.

Of course, the coach tries to help you. But at this level it's very hard to help athletes. My coaches did everything for me with the basics. I had a very good experience as part of the Soviet junior team, and it was also good for my coaches, Viktor Dolidov and Vladimir Vatkin.

Now the motivation comes from me. My dream, my goal is still the Olympics. But before, when I was injured before the 1996 Olympics, it was hard to imagine how I could possibly return and do normal gymnastics again. And I want to thank all the people who were close to me and tried to understand my problem and to help me come back to gymnastics.

When I returned, I knew it would be painful, but I prepared myself for that. I never thought about being world champion after one year. But inside I was thinking to push myself to do more than I could do. It's hard to explain. Maybe it's a feeling you get when you're having a bad experience, not just in gymnastics, but for many reasons. It's a special feeling. ❖

Ivan Ivankov of Belarus won all-around world titles in 1994 and '97.

Opposite & Above: **Ivan Ivankov (Belarus)**

Opposite & Above: **Ivan Ivankov (Belarus)**

A TRANSFORMATION

BY SIMONA AMANAR

GYMNASTICS is a very special sport and it is also a lifestyle. Through gymnastics you experience special situations in which your courage and willpower are tested to the limit. It also requires unusual physical qualities which are at the edge of biomechanical possibilities.

Gymnastics transformed me from a very shy person into a positive, strong and self-confident young lady, and I feel that everything I have done has inspired and motivated me. I feel I am well prepared to face any of the difficulties which may occur in life. It is true that I have sacrificed time and a lot of my energy, both physically and mentally, but I have gained a lot more in return. The effort has been well worth it. I don't think that I lost anything by practising gymnastics and I definitely received a name and the status of a champion in return. There's no doubt that my highest achievement was the Olympic title in Atlanta in '96 and I really fulfilled a dream.

At the moment I am approaching things as they come and

> We have been educated to be a team able to understand and handle failure and success with the same measure.

concentrating only on my training and training-related issues. I believe I am well disciplined and determined not only in training but outside it, as well. I don't give up easily and if I make mistakes I make great efforts to put them behind me and avoid repeating them. I am not a quick learner, but once I have conquered a skill I don't lose it. Usually, I can control my nerves in competition and there are very few situations where I feel butterflies in my stomach. It helps when the crowd support you and most of the time they are very objective. I am happy when I can give them pleasure through my performances.

I am very close to my teammates. We have been educated to be a team able to understand and handle failure and success with the same measure. Only a strong relationship with the coaches and support staff can help you develop into a champion. I know that without them I would not be what I am now. When things are not going well I rely on the patience of my coaches and on my capacity to recover quickly from trouble. In training I need to be committed and to follow all the advice I get from my coaches.

Gymnastics is and certainly will be forever part of my life. I am positive that in the future I will dedicate myself to work as a coach with young girls who wish to become champions.

At the end of the day women's gymnastics is between an art and a science. During these years it was a privilege for me to be part of its development. ❖

Simona Amanar of Romania placed third all-around at the 1996 Olympics, where she also won the gold on vault.

Opposite & Above: **Simona Amanar (Romania)**

A FAMILY AFFAIR

BY JESUS CARBALLO JR.

YMNASTICS has been a way of life for me since I was very young because all my family has been involved in the sport, especially my father. It has been a very positive thing for me to have a family that understands the world of gymnastics, because they can help and support you when things are not going well and it is really nice when you can talk about gymnastics at home and your whole family understands it.

In my opinion the most beautiful part of gymnastics is top level competition and the opportunity to travel the world and meet all kinds of people. But most of all, it brings wonderful moments when I have achieved my goals and made it onto the medal podium.

The most difficult part of the sport is overcoming all the hard times, the injuries, the loss of a coach or a failure in competition. But I also think that the discipline and determination that gymnastics develops helps you to overcome all these problems.

The role of your coach and your relationship with him is cru-

> *It has been a very positive thing for me to have a family that understands the world of gymnastics, because they can help and support you when things are not going well.*

cial because you spend a lot more time with him than with your own family. A coach must be an innovator and a hard worker. He also has to give you confidence in everything he does, and you have to have complete trust in him and know that he believes in your ability and always has your best interests at heart.

Each day the coach and gymnast develop a stronger relationship as friends and work together as a team; in competition they help and support each other so that everything can go to plan. Along with my father, my coach gives me confidence and security every time I get on the apparatus and I always know that my coach wants the best for me.

My relationship with my teammates is good, especially now that we have qualified for the Olympic Games in Sydney and we have a common goal. We help each other as much as we can. I have always been inspired by gymnastics in general and have tried to learn from other gymnasts in order to develop a new and original approach.

I would like to dedicate these lines to my former coach, Marco Antonio Vazquez Moratinos, who died in 1998, because he has been the most important person in my life as a sportsman and I will always appreciate the help and support he gave me that made me a good gymnast. He helped me achieve my ambitions and taught me that if you work every day, the results will follow. ❖

Jesus Carballo of Spain won world titles on high bar in 1996 and '99.

Opposite & Above: **Jesus Carballo (Spain)**

A TEST OF WILL

BY LIU XUAN

YMNASTICS is a kind of sport that combines not only beauty and health but also skill, creativity and innovation. It brings people happiness. Gymnasts can develop an unflinching will and indomitable spirit in the practice of gymnastics.

I have been doing gymnastics for 14 years. The deepest feeling it gives me is that gymnastics can test my will and teach me how to face difficulties and setbacks, it makes me become a person who can think independently and overcome difficulties. At the same time, I have lots of joy in gymnastics. Through gymnastics I understand the happiness of success and the bitterness of failure. My life has become colourful through gymnastics. It is an indispensable part of my life. Because I love gymnastics, there is nothing that I feel is too difficult to endure.

Sometimes I was discouraged, but when I awoke to the fact that I had not achieved my aim, motivation came back to me, I encouraged myself and continued to struggle for my goal to be world champion and win honour for my country. I will always

> *My life has become colourful through gymnastics. It is an indispensable part of my life. Because I love gymnastics, there is nothing that I feel is too difficult to endure.*

keep gymnastics in my heart no matter what I do in the future.

My teammates and I live and train like sisters, caring for each other in everyday life and encouraging each other in competition, because we know that each one of us has made a contribution to our success. We live in harmony.

I am disciplined and have caring coaches. We have good communication and understanding, not only in life but also in training. I also have learned from my coaches how to be a good person, how to treat others and to do things well.

In my opinion, I think qualified coaches should have a sense of responsibility and devotion to their work. And they should also study psychology, because they live with many team members. To think about things from the viewpoint of these children is another important ability. Only with these qualities can a coach work well with young gymnasts.

My whole family gives me great support. My mother used to do gymnastics and my father is a fan of the sport. Although they know the training is very hard, they believe it is important for me to achieve great success without too much struggle. So they give me encouragement in spirit and instruction in training. I could not have achieved my success without the support of my family. I am very grateful to my parents. ❖

Opposite & Above: Liu Xuan (China)

Liu Xuan of China placed seventh all-around at the 1997 World Championships and first on balance beam at the 1998 World Cup.

LOOKING FORWARD

BY KARL LORENZ

am now 14 years old and have taken part in gymnastics since 1987 when I was just three years old. My mother put me into gymnastics to help me develop my coordination and I quickly became attracted to the sport because it was fun and a challenge. Most of all I enjoy performing the flips and somersaults, but of course learning the skills is the hardest part.

Gymnastics keeps me fit and I have learned to concentrate on my routines and not worry about what is going on around me. At the same time I think it is important to focus on your long-term goals and my greatest ambition is to make the Olympic Games and win a gold medal. This year at our national championships we were able to compete in the Sydney SuperDome so I know how exciting it is to compete on the Olympic podium. I was in awe with the sheer size of the competitive arena, and when I closed my eyes I tried to imagine what it would be like with a tense and excited capacity crowd.

My great hero is Vitaly Scherbo. He has achieved world champion status on many occasions along with all his Olympic titles. His skills on the floor and his movements on the parallel bars inspire me greatly. I would like to be just like him.

I have been very fortunate to have three good coaches—Don Pennel, Xu Yu Ting and now Yu Bo—who have helped me toward my best achievements so far, winning the national under-13 and under-15 titles. It was also a great experience for me to compete in the Junior International Canberra Cup and I'm fortunate to have parents and friends who support me in my ambitions.

I would encourage other boys to take up gymnastics because it keeps you fit, gives you a challenge, teaches you self-discipline and it is great fun as well. ❖

Karl Lorenz is a top junior gymnast from Melbourne, Australia.

Left: **Karl Lorenz (Australia) and coach Yu Bo.**
Opposite: **Young Australian gymnast Michael Funnell**

A WAY OF LIFE

Rhythmic gymnasts'
perspectives

A FAIRY TALE

BY ELENA VITRICHENKO

I am now 23 years old, and for 20 of those years I dedicated my life to rhythmic gymnastics. I fell in love with the sport when I was very young. My toys then were the rope, the ball, the hoop, the clubs and at this stage gymnastics was for me nothing but a joyful way of playing. When I discovered that movements combined with music could create beautiful images, gymnastics became my fairy tale.

Later on it turned into a way of assessing my physical and mental capacity and strength. Each time I was able to overcome difficulties and challenges I experienced deep feelings which, I guess, people call happiness. I learned that life cannot be without pressure. If we surrender to pressure in the gym, we will surrender in

> *If we surrender to pressure in the gym,*
> *we will surrender in life.*

life. If we can overcome it in our sport, we can overcome it in life as well.

The support of the audience has always been very important to me, and I am very grateful to all those people who have often approached me to thank me for the pleasure I have given them with my performances and to ask me not to retire. Their support and encouragement have given me the courage to continue to compete and to resist the challenge of the talented youngsters.

I like very much the words of the German philosopher Goethe, who wrote: "Close to my soul are those who seek to achieve the unachievable." My dream is to become Olympic champion and I am following my path toward this dream helped by my coach and mother. ❖

*Previous spread: **Edita Schaufler (Germany)***
*Opposite & Above: **Elena Vitrichenko (Ukraine)***

Elena Vitrichenko of Ukraine won the bronze at the 1996 Olympics and was world champion in 1997.

Opposite & Above: **Elena Vitrichenko (Ukraine)**

Opposite & Above: **Elena Vitrichenko (Ukraine)**

THE ESSENCE OF LIFE

BY ALINA KABAEVA

FOR me rhythmic gymnastics is an art form and the most important force in my life. Through it I can truly express myself, my essence and my emotions in my routines. I compare my sport to ballet. Rhythmic gymnastics represents life itself. It is a quest for something new—a new way of expressing ideas and showing complete mastery of movements, all the things that should be proved in the up-and-coming competitions and most importantly in the Olympic Games.

The most difficult thing is to show the audience and the judges the essence of my routines as I see and understand them. They are not only about a simple combination of particular movements, but are also about my self-expression. It is the combination of these two components that makes the task so challenging.

Since my childhood, when I first took up gymnastics, I liked to see people around during training sessions. When people are able to understand me I receive in return their applause, flowers and even soft toys that cover the floor mat. When I hear the enthusiastic exclamation of my young fans, I know that I have brought my creative ideas to their hearts. This support makes me feel that I am a part of them, that we are together.

The quest for new elements, movements and routines is what I try to contribute to our sport so that rhythmic gymnastics becomes more popular. I would like to see the new elements given the names of the gymnasts who first performed them, as is the tradition in artistic gymnastics.

I will continue to compete while I feel strong; age is not important. I am convinced that rhythmic gymnastics is one of the most difficult sports which demands discipline as a way of life.

A coach and gymnast are components of one and the same unit. To achieve their aim the most important thing for them is to be like-minded people. The main task of the coach is to completely understand the personality of the gymnast and her emotional world, to be able to see her real potential, to develop it and to stick with her until the end of her career.

A good gymnast must have a strong character, self-discipline and excellent health, and these must be maintained carefully. She must be able to overcome difficulties themselves. The rest of the necessary skills can be developed in the process of training. In this respect I consider myself very lucky. When I first met my coach, Irina Viner, she was the coach of world-renowned gymnasts such as Amina Zaripova, Yana Batyrchina and Natalia Lipkovskaya.

Mrs. Viner is, in short, a blacksmith of champions. When I first saw those gymnasts in the training hall, I set myself the aim of achieving results as impressive as theirs. During the training sessions and also outside the gym they helped me to learn a lot. They also showed me how to cope with the most complex elements in my routines. It is not by chance that my coach often says that it is better to see something once than to hear it hundreds of times. I would add that I wish to be like them but at the same time I wish to keep my own individual appeal.

The question of whether rhythmic gymnastics is a life style contains the answer: It is not only a sport, it is the gist of life itself.

Now I am only 16 but my perception of life and people is already much different compared to my recent past. I realise now that I am protected and guided by my coaches and teachers. They give me the chance to achieve top level results. At the same time I feel that I will be able to cope with the difficult situations that may come after my retirement too.

I want to be a leader in sport and also useful in society in general. I wish to be as remarkable as I am in rhythmic gymnastics. I can't think otherwise. ❖

> *It is not only a sport, it is the gist of life itself.*

Opposite: *Alina Kabaeva (Russia)*

Alina Kabaeva of Russia was the 1999 world champion.

Opposite & Above: **Alina Kabaeva** *(Russia)*

Opposite & Above: Alina Kabaeva (Russia)

Opposite & Above: **Alina Kabaeva (Russia)**

Opposite & Above: Eva Serrano (France)

REACHING THE AUDIENCE

BY EVA SERRANO

like my sport because it is very artistic and particularly for the close competition between the gymnasts. Moreover, I enjoy the response of the public and I like using my body and movements to express myself. When I am on the competition floor I always try to convey feelings to the public, such as joy or sadness, and I feel real satisfaction when they respond and I can sense that they have felt a 'shiver' of excitement when I performed.

I think that experience is very important in our sport because you are always aware of the possibilities that could happen during competition and training. I am often very happy in my life, but when there are difficult times in training I try to concentrate on something which makes me feel happy because I know that

I feel real satisfaction when they have felt a 'shiver' of excitement when I performed.

---

there will be more difficult things to face in life. I try to motivate myself by thinking of how much I love my sport.

Each gymnast must have an inherent sense of artistry and a real feeling for the music, but she will need to develop this in her own way and train hard to express herself clearly. I think that every gymnast brings to her sport something different and I think this is in correlation with her unique personality. I try to perform with something different from the others and which is special to me, and the most important aspect for me is that of expression. I try to be a little avant garde in the choice of my music and choreography but it is not always very well accepted by the judges.

Most of all, I like it very much when the audience support me and applaud my performance. At these times I feel carried along by the people, and I love that! ❖

Eva Serrano of France placed fourth at the 1999 World Championships.

Opposite & Above: **Eva Serrano (France) reveals her passion.**

FACE TO FACE

A closer look

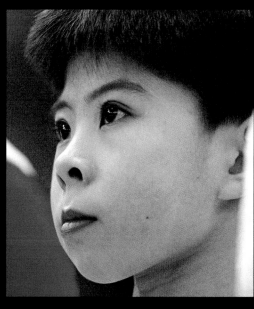

*Far left: **Dominique Dawes (USA)***

Above, clockwise from top left:
Naoya Tsukahara (Japan)
Ioannis Melissanidis (Greece)
Bai Chunyue (China)
Adrienn Varga (Hungary)

Opposite: **Elena Produnova** *(Russia)*
Above: **Svetlana Khorkina** *(Russia)*

"Success is a journey, not a destination."

—*Dominique Dawes (USA)*

Opposite: **Russians Elena Dolgopolova (left) and Svetlana Bakhtina**
Above: **Yuri Chechi (Italy)**

"You need willpower. Without overcoming difficulties, you won't achieve anything."

—*Elena Produnova (Russia)*

Opposite: **Evgenia Pavlina (Belarus)**
Above, clockwise from top left:
Florent Maree (France)
Olga Roschupkina (Ukraine)
Alena Polozkova (Belarus)
Alexei Nemov (Russia)

*Opposite (l-r): **Allana Slater (Australia), Mitja Petkovsek (Slovenia)***
*Above: **Oksana Omelianchik (Ukraine)***

"Failure is part of gymnastics, just like it's part of life. There are high points and low points, struggles and victories."

—*Oksana Omelianchik (Ukraine)*

Opposite: **Elena Zamolodchikova (Russia)**

Above, clockwise from top left:
Andreas Wecker (Germany)
Maria Olaru (Romania)
Yewki Tomita (USA)
Viktoria Karpenko (Ukraine)

PURSUING EXCELLENCE

The role of the coach

MY COACHING PHILOSOPHY

BY LEONID ARKAEV

IT is my strong belief that in modern artistic gymnastics the coach has the primary role and the gymnast the secondary. A real coach needs to have a strong theoretical background and a great ability to work individually with every gymnast. In coaching, you have to consider each gymnast's personality, psychological characteristics, physical condition and other aspects.

For each gymnast a coach has to foresee the results of coaching at each stage of training, and always have reasonable expectations. This would be impossible without the knowledge of developmental trends worldwide, nationally and regionally.

In order to achieve the desired results, careful long-term (for example, a four-year period) and short-term (monthly, weekly, daily) planning has to be done. The purpose of the planning is to set specific goals which must be achieved by a gymnast during a certain period of time. These goals would include technical, phys-

ical and psychological aspects. This should lead to successful and stable performances during important competitions. The actual performance and achievements have to be constantly compared with the goals that were set in the plans, and adjustments should be made if needed.

The coach must set a positive example to the gymnasts regarding the general attitude and devotion toward the training process and gymnastics. Such aspects as discipline, persistence, hard work and human values need to be constantly emphasised. The coach also needs to act as a mentor, explaining the value of doing gymnastics, the role of leading sportsmen in society and the importance of success to the club, the region and the country.

In order to create a serious and intensive training process (taking into consideration the reasonable expectation for each gymnast), positive and negative emotions have to be carefully balanced by a coach. When a gymnast does not take training seriously enough the level of anxiety and responsibility may be raised. When a gymnast does not perform according to expectations, psychological coaching may be appropriate. This may include 'victory story,' its values and benefits. I would like to specifically mention that all the negative emotions which appear during the stressful training process are totally compensated by successful performance at competitions and by newly mastered elements. From the psychological point of view, gymnastics, as any other sport, enables a person to build strong self-confidence and have faith in his or her personal abilities.

The relationship of complete trust between a coach and a gymnast usually develops after several successful competitions. Devoted and loyal relationships in the daily training process are essential for successful performances. Relationship building is a very difficult and important process. It starts with the coach and the coach needs to be a leader. To be trustworthy the coach needs to be honest, fair, consistent, competent and optimistic. Trusting relationships cannot develop if a coach does not have full respect for his gymnasts or does not understand their character, emotion

Opposite: Leonid Arkaev motivates his team at the 1996 Olympics.

> *Devoted and loyal relationships in the daily training process are essential for successful performances.*

and physical abilities and conditions. On a daily basis the coach is responsible for the sporting achievements, safety and education of the gymnasts.

The training of the team of gymnasts starts with the vision and determination of a leading coach among the other coaches of the gymnasts in a team. The team of coaches has to come to a consensus in relation to the assessment of the team level, assessment of main competitor team levels and current development trends in gymnastics. The coaches have to agree on the team planning issues and monitoring process.

Leading gymnasts, in turn, can bring positive or negative assistance in the team training process. It will be positive when they also agree with the approach to training. They need to be convinced that their own performance is highly dependent on the performance of the team as a whole and especially the 'outsiders.' It is important that everyone realises that gymnastics is a team sport. It is also important to create kind, honest and fair relationships among the team members. This needs to be constantly emphasised during and after the workouts. Good relations between the coaches are also essential.

Awards must be granted during daily workouts and after the main competitions. Daily 'awards' come from the satisfaction of successful training. These can be both positive and negative.

Awards granted during significant competitions (Olympic Games, world championships) can be both material and moral, depending on the attitude toward highest sport achievement in each particular country. Personally, for me the most valuable awards are the State Honour medals. I have five of them.

It would be difficult to overestimate the importance of material and technical aspects in modern gymnastics. This relates to the increasing springiness of gymnastics equipment, as well as the usage of fast information, tele- and video-equipment, computer programmes enabling instant analysis to be carried out, interpreting the results immediately and providing the gymnast with the most accurate data. We recommend wide usage of various training aids, the simpler the better.

The future of gymnastics is in searching for and mastering new, bio-mechanically more complicated elements. Creativity of gymnasts and coaches is unlimited as well as their desire for perfection. New elements do not need to bring additional risk and danger. Before the new technical element is to be learned, the physical conditioning of the gymnast must be increased. In this way, injuries will not occur.

Competent, objective and fair operations by the Technical Committees of the FIG are highly beneficial for the future development of gymnastics. These committees need to be well aware of the consequences of their positive and negative decisions.

We can see today that the main direction of gymnastics development is in two areas: 1) increasing complexity and perfection; and 2) in increasing awareness and popularity. This is what the spectator wants. These trends, if continued into future development, will ensure more supporters and admirers of the sport of gymnastics. ❖

Leonid Arkaev is a Merited Coach of Russia and President of the Russian Gymnastics Federation.

Opposite top: **Russian coach Evgeny Nikolko sets the parallel bars.**
Opposite bottom: **Ivan Ivankov (Belarus) gets moral support from Viktor Dolidov.**
Below: **Svetlana Khorkina (Russia) receives the wisdom of Boris Pilkin.**

"Coaches can be likened to roots; you see

the flowers, not the roots."

—*Boris Pilkin (Russia)*

"A coach needs to love gymnastics very much and not count the hours spent in the gym."

—*Tamara Yatchenko (Russia)*

"I am obsessed with beautiful gymnastics."

—*Peggy Liddick (Australian National Coach)*

Opposite: Spanish National Coach Jesus Carballo and Susana Garcia at the 1998 European Championships
Above: Peggy Liddick and Shannon Miller at the 1993 World Championships

Opposite top: **Romanian coach Octavian Belu celebrates a victory.**
Opposite bottom (l-r): **Romanians Gina Gogean, Lavinia Milosovici and Simona Amanar listen intently.**
Above: **Chinese coach Huang Yubin helps Li Xiaoshuang with his grip.**

"You must sacrifice your time to be someone in any activity, whether it is gymnastics or playing the violin. If you are nobody, nobody looks at you."

—*Octavian Belu (Romania)*

"Good coaching is about responsibility."

—*Trevor Low (Great Britain)*

Opposite: Svetlana Kuznetsova (Uzbekistan) nervously watches one of her gymnasts.

Above: 1996 U.S. Olympic assistant Mark Williams stills one of his gymnasts.

Right: 1988 Olympian Ken Meredith (Australia) passes along his experience to one of his club gymnasts.

DEVELOPING ARTISTRY

BY ADRIANA POP

I believe gymnastics starts with choreography, or artistic preparation. Through choreography we can develop body positions, expression, aesthetics, balance, musicality, space orientation and rhythm. If we think, for example, of only floor exercise and balance beam, which are directly connected to artistic preparation, we can observe the importance of choreography.

Artistic preparation truly begins during the gymnast's first six to 12 months in the sport. It must start at a very young age with simple body positions: the legs, arms and head. Simple combinations should be learned next, and then the basics of classical ballet. According to the child's age, there also are exercises of rhythm, balance, flexibility, and for learning to feel different types of music.

When the children have assimilated the first steps, we try combinations and exercises. As they learn, we try to include more difficult elements which are in accordance with the requirements of the Code of Points. All of this artistic preparation has to be within the ability level of the gymnast.

The relationship between the coach and the choreographer is very tight and one of collaboration, understanding and trust. In many situations the coach needs a little spark that we, the choreographer, can find. For example, consider the floor exercise of Lavinia Milosovici at the 1992 Olympics in Barcelona. She performed a little jump at the end of her second tumbling pass which caught the eyes of the judges. Another example is the beam routine of Ludivine Furnon. I needed to add a little part in the exercise, and my husband, Nelu, had the idea of the Shushunova skill. She presented that at the 1997 World Championships, a skill that now bears her name.

Because of my background and professional experience, I prepare gymnasts in three different systems: Romanian, French and American. I have had very good relationships with the coaches in all three systems. The choreographer's job is to create the compositions for floor exercise and balance beam and to develop the correct body positions for all of the events. In this respect, the Code of Points has an important role in requiring the necessary combinations for floor exercise and balance beam.

It is also up to the choreographer to choose the music, another crucial aspect in creating a composition. A good floor exercise must satisfy various criteria: the Code of Points, variety, dynamism and orientation in space. The gymnast must be able to express all of her qualities and also entertain the audience.

Another important role of the choreographer is the creation of the schedules for the warm-up and conditioning. The warm-up at the dance barre can be classical or modified. The warm-up through music can include all kinds of dance and movement, such as jazz, aerobics and flexibility.

For the actual preparation of gymnastics skills, repetition is the key to success. Repeating a simple jump, for example, in a certain time period will produce the desired execution, amplitude and height. Repeating the complex exercises is the only way to reach quality execution. Successful repetition breeds confidence, which makes practices more pleasant. Therefore, from a physical and psychological point of view, the gymnast will feel better prepared in a competitive environment.

One of the most important qualities of a choreographer is the ability to demonstrate a movement. Since I began my career as a choreographer in 1988, I worked shoulder to shoulder with the gymnasts in the warm-ups, at the dance barre, and in the floor routines. Other qualities a choreographer needs include talent,

> *The relationship between the coach and choreographer is very tight and one of collaboration, understanding and trust.*

*Opposite: **Ludivine Furnon (France)***

Your ideas come from inside. You must have a feeling, you must have an inspiration. If you don't, you should not even attempt to choreograph a routine.

imagination, feeling for music, patience, persistence, knowing the rhythm of the social life, originality, confidence and acting. A choreographer also needs to know the personality of each gymnast, and have a feeling for aesthetics, beauty and spontaneity. Here I would like to add that I have a great respect for personalities such as Neschka Robeva, Mikhail Baryshnikov, Maurice Béjart, Steven Spielberg, Coco-Chanel, Nadia Comaneci and Eileen Langsley.

Another very important quality, if you can call it a quality, is love for your job. Choreography, in my opinion, is an art, and like any other art, there are no limits. Your ideas come from inside. You must have a feeling, you must have an inspiration. If you don't, you should not even attempt to choreograph a routine.

Gymnasts are also very different. Therefore, in their prepara-

tion, they need a certain individuality. From this individuality, and with a detailed knowledge of the gymnast, we create a gymnastics 'personality,' a so-called style. I believe you can teach somebody to 'dance,' even if she is stiff as a board.

Since no gymnast—and nobody—is perfect, when I compose a floor routine I try to highlight a gymnast's qualities and hide her negative aspects. Through my compositions, I always try to highlight the personality of each gymnast and coordinate it with the music and her qualities. I also try to make it look genuine, not artificial or out of place.

Because of its direct relationship with artistry, choreography should have a more important role in the future of gymnastics, and also a more objective evaluation in the Code of Points. ❖

Adriana Pop of Romania began her gymnastics career at age five, studying ballet. She competed in rhythmic gymnastics for eight years and began her work as a choreographer in 1988. She has worked with the national teams of Romania, Belgium and France, as well as with national team members in the U.S. She is currently the national team choreographer for France.

Opposite & Below: **Flexibility is stressed at the Special Junior Girls' Olympic Gymnastics School in St. Petersburg, Russia.**

"Artistic perfection is the right of no one. It is hard earned by work, work and more work. Time, care and patient teaching make for fine technique. There are no short cuts, there is no easy way."

—*Rita Bijholt (Holland)*

Opposite: **Dina Kochetkova (Russia)**
Above: **Olga Roschupkina (Ukraine)**

Atlanta 1996

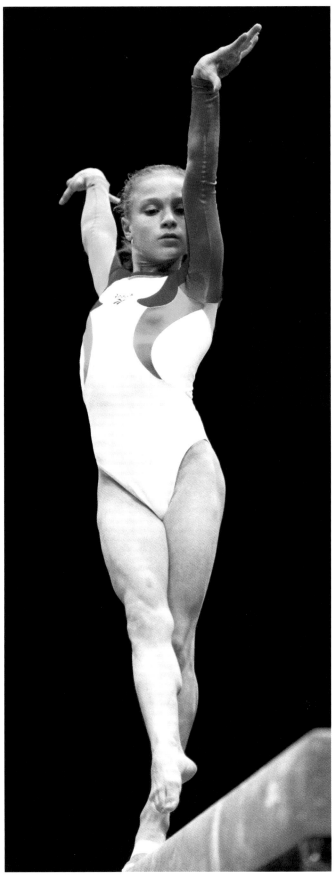

Opposite: Annika Reeder (Great Britain)
Left: Maria Olaru (Romania)
Above: Evgenia Kuznetsova (Russia)

"We have a passion for the sport, a passion for perfection."

—*Muriel Grossfeld (USA)*

"A gymnast must aspire to be an artist as well as an athlete."

—*Dwight Normile (International Gymnast)*

Opposite: **Alexei Nemov (Russia)**
Above: **Oliver Walther (Germany)**

PURSUING EXCELLENCE

The role of the rhythmic coach

THE FUTURE OF RHYTHMIC

BY BIANCA PANOVA

GYMNASTICS has taught me how to face my problems, and to fight to solve them. We are already in the year 2000 and many things have changed in life as well as in sport. To take the right direction for the future we have to look at the past and understand the present. In these lines I would like to share some of my visions of rhythmic gymnastics in the new millennium.

I have always visualised rhythmic competitions as a great spectacle with many effects: costumes, original music with vocals, a special lighting, and of course, male performance. I believe that rhythmic is definitely missing out from new developments since it is only for women.

Despite the theory that rhythmic is the most feminine sport and that adding men will destroy this image, I dare to claim that the grace and femininity would be even more notable against the background of male performance. Both artistic gymnastics and figure skating are excellent examples of this.

In the past, striving for results could lead to lack of attention to the preparation and creation of the rhythmic gymnast. In the 1980s, the workout and training were very specific to rhythmic, without using the resources of other sports such as athletics, weight lifting and swimming, which have the ability to build some of the basic motion qualities of the gymnast, such as power and resistance. On this basis, the gymnast can express her technical and emotional talent on a completely new level. That can happen only if she is free from physical effort and technical difficulties. In my opinion, the rhythmic gymnast must be a versatile, developed athlete. She has not only to impress, but also to touch the people.

Not enough time and attention was paid to nutritional sport supplements and diets for the gymnasts. That is why many of them appeared painfully weak. This led to different injuries and unwanted changes in the bone structure of the body. Today there are plenty of products which, when scientifically applied, can supply the sporting body with all the necessary vitamins, minerals and micro-elements needed to improve the metabolism, support the body with building and energy supplying materials and boost the athlete's performance. Today could be a song to the gymnast: to be powerful but also slim, elegant and flexible.

The relationship between coach and gymnast has been and always will be a delicate one. But exactly here is the trick. The heavy training schedule places great demands on maintaining mutual respect, a good feeling, trust and understanding between them. This is mostly dependent on the coach and comes from his or her human intelligence, psychological knowledge and understanding of the mind of the gymnast. That is why, when the coach has been a top gymnast, it can only help her to recognize and control the extreme loading during the training period. Of course, the gymnast has to be clever enough to understand that she cannot reach the top alone, she cannot train alone, and when she touches success, she should not forget all those people who helped her.

> *She has not only to impress, but to touch people.*

So, if I have to describe the gymnast of the new millennium, there are a few words: a woman, a universal athlete, a healthy and motivated person with a kindly soul and a big heart.

I am convinced that with much love and dedication we could make rhythmic a unique sport that knows no difference between aesthetics and emotion, between art and joy, which awakens your senses and does not allow a merely neutral response.

Rhythmic is before all a feeling. Close your eyes, take a deep breath, feel the music and start to draw with your body. Discover and express your identity. You can laugh, you can cry, you can joke with the audience and be real. The audience will appreciate your truth and will reward you with their spontaneous applause, the biggest gift and sometimes better than a gold medal. ❖

Bianca Panova of Bulgaria won all five individual gold medals at the 1987 World Championships. Now she is a coach in Belgium.

Previous spread: **Russian group**
Above: **Bianca Panova (Bulgaria)**

Russian gymnasts Natalia Lipkovskaya (above) and Alina Kabaeva (opposite) receive technical advice and emotional support, respectively.

"You must be who you are."

—Irina Viner (Russia)

"Once you have felt it, you cannot forget it and you always want to feel it."

—*Bianca Panova (Bulgaria)*

A young gymnast perhaps dreams of one day reaching the level of Irina Tchatchina of Russia (opposite).

WORKING AS ONE

BY MISAKO GOMEI

I believe there is no inherent difference in coaching the development of skill in individuals and groups. If the coach loves the sport and has a clear vision, both aspects are the same. Speaking of technique, when I teach individual gymnasts I try to draw out their potential ability and their character as best I can. When I teach a group I try to pull out not only each gymnast's character but also the group 'colour,' which is a combination of the five different personalities. I also try to choreograph and develop a mix of combinations that best illustrates what makes that group special, a routine that is peculiar to them.

Unlike individual gymnasts, group gymnasts need to be cooperative, to trust each other and not become critical of each other or irritated during a performance. These qualities are needed

---

Group gymnasts need to be cooperative, to trust each other.

---

because the mistake of one becomes the failure of the group. In other words, all the group members have to cover one mistake and make a success out of cooperating together. This special quality must be developed by daily training and by learning to feel for each other and the challenges they are facing.

In 1999 the Japanese group competing in the World Championships in Osaka qualified for the Olympic Games for the first time. The confidence in their skills and technique and their trust in each other had been developed by daily training. Also, the mental techniques taught by their mental trainer brought their ability and potential into full play under great pressure and in front of a home crowd. This could not have been possible without the cooperation of all the group members. ❖

Above: **Japan**
Opposite: **Spain**

Misako Gomei has been Head Coach of the Japanese rhythmic group since 1993.

Hungary

Opposite: **Russia**
Below: **North Korea**

"Risk is part of the beauty of gymnastics."

—Maria Fernandez (Spanish group coach)

Top: **Kazakhstan**
Above: **Ukraine**
Opposite: **Russia**

"Subtle choreography and perfect harmony between pure gymnastic gesture and the technical mastering of the apparatus. Spirit and content unite in an exclusive art which expresses talent, imagination and femininity."

—*World of Gymnastics, No. 17*

ART IN ACTION

Judges' perspectives

BALANCING ART AND SPORT

BY JEFF THOMSON

PERHAPS no activity relies more on the skill of balance than the sport of artistic gymnastics. The gymnasts themselves must almost always strive for equilibrium in their movement performance. The coaches too must strive for balance. A balance between the need to push the athlete toward greater achievements and the need to achieve both physical and psychological well being. The coach must also watch for a balance between art and sport, as gymnastics is truly both. I feel very strongly that, as a judge, I too must achieve a balance. The same balance in many ways, as both the coach and athlete must feel. We must, as judges, consider the need for the sport to progress and develop with regard to new elements and techniques and the need to evaluate both fairly and accurately the performance. We must try to balance our role as an aloof third party responsible for results/outcomes and as a crucial part of the athletes' performance-enhancing feedback loop. Perhaps more than any other sport, we must look for a balance in evaluation between art and sport, the aesthetic and the objective.

As judges we often play an important role in setting the direction in which gymnastics will go. I remember clearly the first time I saw Valery Liukin perform both his triple back somersault on floor exercise and his Tkachev with a full twist on high bar (movements now named in his honour). In both instances the aesthetic performances were not perfect. However, the recognition that these movements were exceptional for their technical preparation and were clearly pushing forward the boundaries of difficulty allowed one, with a clear conscience, to say, "It is not only acceptable but perhaps necessary to 'forgive' these small aesthetic shortcomings in favour of pushing the sport forward." It was a balancing between the need to have the sport progress and evaluating perfect aesthetic execution. We have since seen absolutely per-

fect execution of both these super elements!

It seems to me that it is an athlete's nature to strive for Faster, Higher, Stronger, the Olympic creed. What of art? To me, a perfect score of 10—in execution—can represent the achievement of art. Not all gymnasts can, for a variety of reasons, perform the most difficult elements. Nor perhaps is that their ambition. But if a gymnast achieves perfection in execution, for one brief moment at least, then he will have risen to the level of art.

It was this aspect of gymnastics, perhaps more than any other, which attracted me in the first place. The idea that it was simply me working with the apparatus in an attempt to see how close I could come to mastery of performance. From a judging perspec-

> *If a gymnast achieves perfection in execution, for one brief moment at least, then he will have risen to the level of art.*

tive it is also this same idea which motivates and excites me. For, whatever the level of competition, either beginners or at the Olympic Games, I have always seen my role as being responsible for informing the gymnast, through my score, how close they have come toward mastery and perfection, and therefore art.

As a judge I strive to present myself as someone the coaches and gymnasts could rely on for an accurate assessment of their work. I would hope to be regarded not as something or someone they are competing against, but simply as another source of assistance for them in trying to gain mastery of the apparatus. I suppose that I perceive myself as an objective third party when I am

Opposite: Huang Liping (China) displayed high levels of virtuosity and difficulty to win the world title on parallel bars in 1994.

judging. The person responsible for saying how close to perfection the gymnast has come, to determine that a particular routine was 9.4 or 94 percent or even 9.9 or 99 percent. This, of course, begs the question, What is perfection? What is truly worth a 10 or 100 percent?

A friend of mine, Pierre Claval, a Canadian Olympian who went on to become an FIG judge, once told me that for him to give a perfect score he would have to award virtuosity. For him to give virtuosity, he said, he would have to be "moved" by the routine. He went on to explain that he could be moved by the entire routine or at least some significant part of it. This made complete sense to me, as a judge. I know that I am moved by one of two things in a performance. First, it could be for a purely physical accomplishment. In other words, there were single skills, or sequences for that matter, which were performed in such a way as they seemed to defy nature. Incredible height on a skill or phenomenal strength shown, for example. Second, it could come from a purely emotional sensation. A sense of simply being overcome by the beauty of the movement. I guess, in a way, that is what keeps me judging. I am waiting and hoping to personally witness and be a small part of recognising and acknowledging virtuous perfection.

It is also interesting to consider the concept of the aesthetic and

> *One cannot perform today's most difficult elements in a haphazard way.*

its relationship to difficulty. A student of the philosophy of aesthetics will recognise the link between technical execution and the aesthetic. One cannot perform today's most difficult elements in a haphazard way. By and large, the more difficult the skill performed, the more likely it is for the technical execution to be excellent and for the performance to have therefore automatically achieved an aesthetic quality. I believe that this is one of the major reasons people are so impressed by super elements. They not only have a physical presence to them, but they also possess those magical qualities of grace, beauty and control inherent in aesthetic performance.

*Opposite: **Li Donghua (Switzerland) won the Olympic pommel horse gold because of his superb execution.***

*Above: **Head judge Julio Marcos (Spain) confers with the other panellists.***

That is not to say that the more simple elements cannot also be incredibly aesthetic. We often hear the loudest applause at a competition when the gymnast performs even a simple dive roll. I can still clearly picture the wonderful floor routines of the Japanese of the '60s and '70s, Sawao Kato and Akinori Nakayama, for example. Personally, I have always felt that we should be able to award virtuosity bonus points for the elegant and aesthetic execution of these simple elements. That is, if they move us either physically or emotionally.

Clearly the sport of gymnastics is always evolving. One of the greatest challenges will be to balance the need for even greater objective evaluation and the need to somehow recognise and evaluate the expressive, artistic aspects. In my opinion, it would be a shame if all we looked for or attempted to evaluate were the purely technical aspects of the routine. If we do not acknowledge—and embrace—the expressive and artistic side of gymnastics, we risk losing it.

The incredibly complex task of evaluating a gymnast's performance is made all the more difficult by having to balance the need for the sport to move forward, in terms of difficulty, with the need to acknowledge and reward artistry. All of this must occur within the constraints of objectivity and fairness. However, I sincerely believe that if the judging community is perceived as a crucial part of the gymnasts' development, in their quest to gain mastery of the apparatus and their own bodies, then the task can be tremendously rewarding and satisfying, as it always has been for me. ❖

International judge Jeff Thomson of Canada is President of the Men's Technical Assembly of the Canadian Federation.

Opposite: Szilveszter Csollany (Hungary) shows superlative strength during this inverted cross.

Above: Erick Lopez (Cuba) possesses an ideal body for gymnastics: light and strong.

France's Benjamin Varonian (left) and Canada's Kris Burley (opposite) create an illusion of sorts as they drop into a skill invented by Germany's Sven Tippelt.

"If you reduce gymnastics to its numerical evaluations, you lose its essence."

—*Brian Cazeneuve (Sports Illustrated)*

JUDGING RHYTHMIC

BY EGLE ABRUZZINI

RHYTHMIC gymnastics took its place in the FIG programme long before it became an independent sport. Already at the Melbourne Olympic Games in 1956, rhythmic gymnastics formed part of the gymnastic women's team event. The first international competition was organised in 1963 in Budapest, but it was only after the Havana World Championships in 1971 that rhythmic gymnastics had its own technical committee and president, Professor Andreina Gotta, the first rhythmic gymnastics-FIG president and, thus, became the third sporting discipline of the FIG.

The main features which distinguish rhythmic gymnastics from the other FIG disciplines are:

It is this very aesthetic and artistic tendency that makes rhythmic gymnastics particularly attractive to the general public.

• the use of small pieces of hand apparatus (rope, hoop, ball, clubs and ribbon)
• the absence of acrobatics, at least that of extreme difficulty
• a continuous search for aesthetic and artistic movements

It is this very aesthetic and artistic tendency that makes rhythmic gymnastics particularly attractive to the general public. The ability, skills, qualities and physical effort required to perform expressive and aesthetic exercises render this form of gymnastics especially appealing and enjoyable as a fine dancing display.

The place occupied by rhythmic gymnastics in the Olympic programme is still not totally satisfactory, both because of the lack of a final competition for single pieces of apparatus in the individual and team events but also because of the low number of participants (24 individual gymnasts and 10 groups). Whilst these numbers ensure extremely high technical standards, they

also discourage many federations from allocating to rhythmic gymnastics the financial and human resources needed for the growth in their countries. I do not believe it is going to be easy to obtain anything more for rhythmic gymnastics; the current sports policy of the International Olympic Committee is that of limiting and reducing the number of sports and participants. Our efforts in this sphere will not, however, be lacking.

Rhythmic gymnastics is a demanding sport, both physically and technically. It can, of course, be performed "just for fun," for one's health and physical and mental well-being, and for such activity no special qualities are needed. It is not hard to get into either and is very often included in general gymnastics events.

High level activity is another story. Rhythmic gymnastics requires qualities that are out of the ordinary and at a certain point cannot be trained. Think, for example, about flexibility. As motor specialists know, to attain a level of flexibility suitable for the requirements of this sport, inborn structural qualities are needed regarding joints, tendons and muscles. But when one comes across a gymnast possessing such natural flexibility, a great advantage on the one hand, there is the opposite problem: that of controlling such suppleness. This type of gymnast must go through general toning work to develop proper body alignment in order to build up the other necessary properties such as the explosive power needed for leaps, which must express not only a high elevation but also a great breadth of form.

The balances and pirouettes and the other major body movements typical of rhythmic gymnastics require considerable technical preparation and long, demanding training sessions. It is not

Opposite: Amina Zaripova (Russia) goes behind the back.

an easy task, bearing in mind the difficulty of body movements, the need for considerable skills, coordination and the cohesion of apparatus handling with those of the body, rhythmic sensibility to bind and coalesce complex movements with music, and a highly developed aesthetic sense and expressive capacity to perform the whole routine as a harmonious unit. Rhythmic gymnasts all have their own particular skills and qualities which gradually emerge, and they remain as a lasting gift, even at the conclusion of competitive activity, above all a harmonious physical development that renders these gymnasts really "beautiful."

As in all sports centring on quality, rhythmic judges have an important and difficult role to play. The assessment of routines requires a great ability to perceive and recognise the difficulties that come very quickly, one after another, and sometimes almost imperceptibly during the execution of an exercise. Therefore, it is not enough for a rhythmic judge to have the correct competence and aptitude; he or she must also have continuous experience in the field and resort to the analysis of videos. Competence, aptitude and constant training are qualities that are even more indispensable for the group exercise, which multiplies difficulties by five. In my humble opinion, this programme warrants all the efforts that are put in, because it is the most beautiful, spectacular, varied and typical rhythmic gymnastics activity. The spectacle described above is indeed enriched by the choreographic possibilities offered to a group of five gymnasts and five pieces of apparatus (and sometimes two different pieces in the same routine), working in elegant collaboration.

What has rhythmic gymnastics meant to my life? It has been a great part of it. In addition to the almost 20 years of activity with the FIG technical committee, in Italy I began to work in this magnificent form of gymnastics in 1962, first as an instructor at the Higher Institute of Physical Education, then as a coach and federation official. An entire existence indeed!

I have been asked what sort of contribution I have made to this sport. It is difficult to say. It is up to others to say whether I have left any mark on the sport at the end of my active involvement. What I can say is that I have received a lot from this activity, from everybody—including gymnasts—with whom I have worked. I have grown together with rhythmic gymnastics and have seen it grow, perhaps helping it on its way, from an educational and aesthetic motor activity to a sport that has reached high technical standards.

Rhythmic gymnastics can, of course, grow further. It has great potential because it is a little less risky than other forms of gymnastics, it requires minimum, low-cost apparatus and can be performed in spaces that do not need to be specific to this sport. In many countries and clubs, rhythmic gymnastics is being practised by a growing percentage of gymnasts who prefer it to other forms of gymnastics. This, however, is not sufficient to consolidate international success. It should be credible as a sport and everyone's contribution is needed: that of coaches, who must render routines easier to interpret; of judges, who must always make their judgements fair and comprehensible; and above all, of enthusiasts. The reform of the rules in 2001 is moving in this direction. Let us hope that it achieves its purpose.   ❖

Egle Abruzzini of Italy is the Rhythmic Technical Committee President of the Fédération Internationale de Gymnastique.

*Opposite: **Alba Caride Costas (Spain) hits all the right angles.***
*Above: **Olga Belova (Russia) over extends herself.***

"The whole art of gymnastics comes down to this: We are under the illusion that everything flows from the source, that art is easy, so perfect is the mastery of the body and gesture. At that moment we forget the hours, days, years of tedious training … to see nothing more than lightness, facility and the supernatural grace of these young women."

—*Philippe Barraud (L'Hebdo, Switzerland)*

Opposite: **Italy, like spokes of a wheel or perhaps a budding flower.**

Above: **A little drama from Jessica Howard (USA)**

*Two exceptional leaps from Ukraine's Anna Bessonova
(opposite) and Japan's Sae Takahashi (above)*

OUTSIDE IN *The media*

CENTENAIRE

ART, MIND AND MUSCLE

BY JOHN CRUMLISH

OMPELLING for its synergy of visual aesthetics, physical dynamics and psychological tactics, gymnastics offers ever-evolving interest and intrigue to first-time spectators, avid fans and duty bound media alike.

Because gymnasts perform routines—rather than simply aim, throw or dash toward a finish line—their performances are often assessed by media with the adjective-abundant drama and scrutiny of a theatre or film review. Few athletic events offer as much potential for beauty, danger and both. Ostensibly foolhardy physical manoeuvres send gymnasts hurling into precariously beautiful body positions, as they leap, twist and flip—courage, kinetics and passion aloft.

Gymnasts astound, entertain and inspire because they make their esoteric talents seem simultaneously simple and impossible. Observers are usually amazed, often charmed and sometimes even frightened by extraordinary contortions, spins and combinations thereof. Culled from a lexicon that includes the Khorkina, the Guczoghy and the Omelianchik, these tricks can be as intimidating as the champion gymnasts who invent them.

Because gymnasts are encouraged to infuse their performances with personality, the sport's most successful stars are both irresistibly intangible and endearingly human.

Russia's Svetlana Khorkina entices journalists, photographers and television cameramen with the provocative facial, physical and vocal expressiveness of the sport's sex symbol she has become, since winning the 1996 Olympic title on uneven bars, the 1997 world all-around championship and the 1998 European crown.

Through his brash performances, gestures and self-assessments, bulky Russian expatriate Dmitry Karbanenko of France pointedly vindicates himself from rejections of the past by lumbering his French team toward medal contention in 2000.

Idolatry and plaudits, however, are shifted and snatched away by the slightest quiver on the balance beam or twitch of the torso ... on the rings.

Elfin Olga Roschupkina of Ukraine handles her status as a possible candidate to bring her country its third Olympic all-around gold medal in as many Olympiads with stern self-assurance on the podium and giggly teenage self-consciousness off it.

Greece's elegant Ioannis Melissanidis, 1996 Olympic champion on floor exercise, portrays his athletic quests, defeats and triumphs as scenarios in a modern Greek tragedy.

Idolatry and plaudits, however, are shifted and snatched away by the slightest quiver on the balance beam or twitch of the torso during a handstand on the rings. In perhaps no other sport can infamy and oblivion be sealed by such minute and oftentimes visually incalculable factors.

Because the multiple-judge panel differentiates competitors to a thousandth of a point, a sigh inducing sway can tip the leader off the medal podium, where a worthier and steadier champion eagerly takes his or her place.

Fresh icons emerge, heroes fall and re-emerge. Volition and bravery manifest themselves in whirling, revolving or static displays that at once demand and defy description. For dedicated media, it is both a challenge and a privilege to witness, analyse and share the sport's fascinating synthesis of art, mind and muscle.

Nearly everybody has teetered across a fence railing or swung on playground monkey bars. While the juvenile abandon of such informal gymnastics is long abandoned by most, awe strikes spectators of all age and adroitness as champion gymnasts display their fearless physiological powers. Imaginations soar with the athletes who defy gravity as they gracefully negotiate incredible

*Previous spread: **Media frenzy following U.S. women's triumph in Atlanta***

*Opposite: **Svetlana Bakhtina (Russia)***

combinations of space, angles and directions.

Encouraging more than passing enthusiasm for these feats are the unique physical, technical and personality traits that distinguish each gymnast. Preschoolers and grandparents alike refer simply to "Olga" (Korbut), "Nadia" (Comaneci) and "Lilia" (Podkopayeva), the emotional connotations of such assumed familiarity as lucid and appealing as the first names themselves.

Media constantly introduce the world to—and reacquaint it with—vicarious little sisters, big brothers, children and grandchildren. Even coaches can assume parental and peer identities.

Russia's Leonid Arkaev, his gruff face in a steady scowl as he paces the sidelines during competition, was unable to contain his mirth and pride just hours later while dancing to techno music with his gymnastics "daughters" at the 1998 European Championships banquet.

Ukraine's Galina Losinskaya shared a globally broadcast yet

"I always want to perform with joy. When I'm no longer able to smile, that will be the end of my gymnastics career."

---

tearfully silent hug at the conclusion of the 1996 Olympic all-around final with her victorious protégé Lilia Podkopayeva, whom she calls "my second daughter."

Bela Karolyi, the gregarious ex-Romanian who moulded Nadia Comaneci and Mary Lou Retton to Olympic all-around golds in 1976 and 1984, respectively, has cultivated celebrity status himself with his camera-conscious antics and boisterous diatribes.

While retaining an officially impassive distance as they convey factual information, media also magnify and amplify gymnastics' monumental moments. Audiences wept with Olga Korbut in 1972 and winced with Kerri Strug in 1996—their respective heroics captured instantly on camera and eternally in print and on film.

Triumphs and heartbreaks are flickers in what can be a blurred decade of unheralded toil that comprises a gymnast's career. By illuminating the human emerged from the athlete through profiles, interviews and exposes, media reinforce the validity of such widely witnessed flashes. In doing this, media encourage fan following on an intimate—and therefore more meaningful—level.

Media also present the world with a cast of gymnastics characters as complex and intriguing as their routines.

Svetlana Korkhina (Russia)

Belarus' Vitaly Scherbo, six-time gold medallist at the 1992 Olympics, was as brilliant on the equipment as he was arrogant off it—even swaggering into one post-event press conference toting a can of beer in each of his callused hands.

Roza Galieva, pawn in an internal power play that put eventual champion Tatiana Gutsu in Galieva's rightful all-around slot in 1992, cried bitterly and openly four years later amid the pro-American hysterics in Atlanta. Several months later at a Moscow competition, I approached Galieva for an interview for *International Gymnast* magazine. Slightly apprehensive because I perceived her to be a justifiably guarded young woman, I was delighted by her immediate amenability and pleasant frankness.

I first interviewed Svetlana Khorkina during the 1994 World Championships in Germany. Then a gangly 15-year-old who had only recently debuted as the sport's diva-to-be, Khorkina had one hand on her hip, the other hand in constant motion as she gestured whilst she spoke, and both of her poignant Russian eyes riveted on mine throughout. I was very impressed by Khorkina's certitude and flippancy, with which she has indulged me to ever-evolving degrees at competitions around the world since.

Journalists must often be as deft and pliant as their gymnastics subject, while relationships are established, reinforced and even challenged. Gymnasts can be modest or outspoken, but tend to be less media-savvy than their counterparts in other high-profile (albeit high-income) sports. Female gymnasts, mostly in their mid-teens, can be particularly obsequious or anxious when probed by the most innocuous of questions about their gymnastics or personal life.

Media gain gymnasts' confidence and their own credibility not only by the timing of their queries, but by delivering them in a manner that is both direct and non-threatening. Whether pre-arranged or impromptu, journalistic 'ambushes' and the exchanges which ensue can be mellow, frenetic, languid or feisty—given the right timing, spacing and chemical synergy between journalist and athlete. A gymnast tends to respect a journalist's mission when the journalist recognises the gymnast's need to prioritise and focus in the course of competition. This equilibrium invariably establishes a fair ground for mutually beneficial interchange.

For as many interviews I have conducted in ordinary settings such as hotel lobbies and training gyms, I have conducted successful ones in atypical venues: Russia's enigmatic Elena Dolgopolova, slouched next to me on a rumbling bus in St. Petersburg; Dina Kochetkova, on a grassy slope during a noisy outdoor banquet in San Juan; Canada's Yvonne Tousek, kneaded by a masseur during a rubdown, from the doorway of a training room in Texas; Olga Roschupkina, all-around leader of the victo-

Top: **The U.S. men's team steps into the Olympic arena—and into the spotlight—at Atlanta '96.**

Opposite: **1996 Olympic all-around champion Lilia Podkopayeva (Ukraine)**

"*I'm still the same Lilia, just like before. People remind me that I'm the Olympic champion but I haven't changed.*"

rious Ukrainian junior team at the 1998 European Championships, surrounded in the stands by her cheering compatriots as the senior event got under way; the Uzbekistan women's team, attentive, but occasionally distracted by the comedy programme playing silently on the TV in the corner of their hotel room; Russia's Alexei Bondarenko, fighting with his new fame as 1997 national champion, from the confines of a plastic chair in the stands of Moscow's immense Olympic complex. Intimate moments and feelings sometimes avail themselves unprovoked. Some are delightful, others poignant, still others tragic.

Gymnastics, a sport whose participants and fans span from Iceland to Namibia, retains global interest because fascination with its beauty and boldness is universal. Fledgling programmes are launching on every continent, determined to challenge the traditional monoliths—among them the theatrical Russians, pragmatic Romanians and precise Chinese.

Further spreading and illuminating the sport's worldwide appeal, the influence of many prominent coaches and even their former star gymnasts is transcending indigenous boundaries. Today, Chinese coaches are commissioned to work with the national teams of France and Australia. Ukrainians and Belarusians oversee clubs in Brazil. Russians flourish in Canada, Texas, California and Tennessee. Romanians rule programmes in the British Isles. This dissipation of talent provides access to heretofore covert professional perspectives, athletic techniques and cultural nuances.

Now more than ever before in the history of gymnastics, the blotting of national borders has accentuated and enriched the sport. Old foes are new allies; past secrets are now published agendas. The exciting dividend for the world's gymnastics enthusiasts is multi-cultural gymnastics, soulfully fortified by style and pride unique to the individual nation that the gymnasts represent.

Historically, political allegiances have insinuated themselves in sports whose participants are objectively stratified by subjective (and at times, misguided) individual judges. Dubious scores create media scandals that draw attention to gymnastics, yet undermine the sport's credibility and pelt its athletes' psyches. At the 1966 World Championships in Dortmund, German print journalists exposed a scoring inequity against American Doris Brause, with a bold front-page report. ABC television relayed a similar injustice against Kathy Johnson during the 1978 World Championships in France, via live transmission of the event-halting, shrill audience protest.

While retaining their official neutral stance, journalists sometimes exploit their watchdog status to challenge apparent ethics

Left: 1994 & '97 world all-around champion Ivan Ivankov (Belarus)

Opposite: Alexei Bondarenko (Russia)

Former "boy wonders" Ivan Ivankov of Belarus and Alexei Bondarenko of Russia have developed into hardy leading men, hurling into a Sydney contest that promises the most drama and diversity in Olympic gymnastics history.

violations. At the 1994 World Championships in Germany, American Shannon Miller received an ostensibly generous score after missing an element in her routine on the uneven bars. A questionably high score resulted, launching vocal audience protest and a tempestuous inquisition of a tactful judges' representative by a smoky roomful of international journalists. This confrontation was rendered even more contentious, since the official was also American. The justification of Miller's score made worldwide sports pages, many of which ran cynical reports of the apparent judging manipulations.

So what of the future? Every four years the International Gymnastics Federation revises its Code of Points, which outlines and even dictates elements, combinations and values of routines on each apparatus. Inherent to the Code—in any incarnation—are argument inducing policies relating to technical requirements, and even the minimum age of participation in international com-

petition. Supporters defend such modifications in the name of safety, healthy gymnast development and rejuvenated public interest in the sport, while detractors complain of seemingly arbitrary edicts which discourage creativity and diminish audience enthusiasm.

Nevertheless, gymnasts continue to fervently negotiate and stretch the Code, to ensure the sport's future is as legendary as its past and as fresh as its present. Distinguished from typically petite counterparts by their womanly physiques, taller athletes such as Russia's Svetlana Khorkina and Hungary's Adrienn Varga have manipulated the new rules to crowd-pleasing levels as glamorous as they are triumphant. 1996 Russian Olympian Evgenia Kuznetsova retains her tiny frame, but glides into Sydney with aesthetics cultivated and stimulated by maturity. Former "boy wonders" Ivan Ivankov of Belarus and Alexei Bondarenko of Russia have developed into hardy leading men, hurling into a Sydney contest that promises the most drama and diversity in Olympic gymnastics history.

Much of the world "discovered" gymnastics when they watched television broadcasts or read front-page stories about Soviet sweetheart Olga Korbut's exploits during the 1972 Olympics. Korbut's emotionally enhanced performances jolted the sport into marquee status at future games; when tickets went on sale for the 1996 Games in Atlanta, six of every 10 requests were for gymnastics. Thousands of spectators paid just to attend training sessions.

The conquest of the Atlanta Olympiad by the U.S. women's team inspired their victory-conscious American fans and frustrated their rivals, while some of the more slanted media coverage

*Above (l-r): **Monique Nuijten (Holland), Yvonne Tousek (Canada)***
*Opposite: **Jaycie Phelps (USA)***

exasperated global audiences. Indeed, the 2000 Games are destined to ignite sportsmanlike vengeance, further intensified by challenges from an expanded roster of recently competitive threats including Spain, Italy, Great Britain, Canada and home team Australia.

These newer contenders have stealthily solidified their prospects throughout the 1997-2000 cycle—undistracted by externally imposed burdens such as unrealistically lofty expectations, nostalgic comparisons to past triumphs and over-exposure. The French women's team, for example, has basked in residual praise following its emergence prior to the 1996 Games. Its senior and junior male counterparts, however, have realised a legitimate

claim by swiping the 1998 European team title from Russia—on Russian turf.

Tempering media proclivity to hype Olympic front-runners are career-stalling variables such as injury, anaemic finances, physical fatigue or simple burn-out. Unpredictable negatives aside, however, the pre-Games hustle for medal candidacy is always a supple thrill, as the sport's leading contenders squeeze, push, pluck and rise above the pack.

At Sydney, gymnastics history will pivot on their agility and fragility. They will spin charms that enrapture the audience of the world. They will compel and inspire the journalists and broadcasters of the world. They will become the legacies of the 2000 Olympic Games.   ❖

John Crumlish, who resides in Los Angeles, has been a contributing writer for International Gymnast *since 1982.*

OUTSIDE IN

Rhythmic media

RHYTHMIC FASCINATION

BY NADINE BLASER

ANCE, art or sport? Rhythmic gymnastics ran under various headings before establishing itself as an Olympic sports discipline. Do you remember the beginning of rhythmic gymnastics? Dance school teachers and directors opposed the formality of the ballet system. American Isadora Duncan, the Austrian choreographer Rudolf Von Laban, Mary Wigman and the liberated dancer Irene Popard were the precursors to a discipline called "modern gymnastics." When this discipline of the '70s made a turn toward becoming a sports discipline, rhythmic gymnastics settled in its present form. Consequently, it positioned itself at the crossroads of sport and art.

Rhythmic gymnastics has become an exclusively female discipline in the world of sport. It is a sport in that it responds to the demands of certain regulations, seeks performance in the taking of risks, technical precision and the speed of execution as well as in compositional originality, and it maintains a ranking system. Yet in this world of popular sports, specifically in the sphere of gymnastics, rhythmic gymnastics determines to remain well positioned as an exclusively female discipline. Of course, men have also participated (both at university level in France and Japan), but in the light of the present Code of Points, the male lacks the place he once had. The beautiful slim and delicate bodies, the gymnast's natural elegance, the expressive faces, the feminine grace in all its splendour and the extraordinary flexibility of the athlete all contribute to the positive nature of the sport.

Aesthetic in nature, rhythmic gymnastics remains above all an artistic composition in the service of sports performance—a sport-art. This sport-art relationship controlled by regulations

This sphere of beauty is in constant harmony within the context of a performance.

urges gymnastics to resolve two essential problems: the dynamics of apparatus handling and body movement in rhythmic variations. The matter at hand deals with the organisational strategy of gymnastic productions which seduce, impress and fascinate judges and the public. Could this sport also have an affinity with the theatrical arts mentioned by Elena Bystritskaya, president of the Soviet Rhythmic Gymnastics Federation in 1984? Compositions with hand apparatus are "real artistic creations" adapted to the technical and artistic Code of Points requirements and with a single goal: seduction.

This sphere of beauty is in constant harmony within the context of a performance. Technical feats with the apparatus, purity of movement, extensive body flexibility, rapidity in execution, originality of composition, risks and artistic interpretation blend together when the apparatus and the gymnast harmonise to relay a story, a theme, music, the artistic selection of a leotard, colours closely related to the artistic communication of the composition.

In short, rhythmic gymnastics is multifaceted. By its numerous fashions of technical and artistic expression, it fascinates, arouses emotion and calls out to the spectator from its affecting dimension. How can one help being moved by the performance of Lilia Ignatova (Bulgaria) with the ball in the 1983 World Championships in Strasbourg, when she used the theme from the song *"Ne me quitte pas!"* (Don't leave me) by Jacques Brel. Beside her red ball she was, for a moment, a bewitching enchantress.

Rhythmic gymnastics is a sport-art appreciated by the media. "A festival of grace and harmony," "Dream Gymnastics," "Magical," etc. The press does not skimp on words. This sport-art mixture is well known and rhythmic gymnastics has finally succeeded in its challenge, for it seems impossible to devote so much media coverage to a multi-faceted sport. And yet...

The world championships in Strasbourg was a starting point

Previous spread: **Amina Zaripova (Russia)**
Opposite: **Larissa Lukyanenko (Belarus)**

for a national, and eventually international, promotion of gymnastics. More than 10 years later, France welcomed a second world championships to its capital. It was a quality event, covered by the media and broadcast by various TV channels. "RSG, Grace, Rapture, Symphony." Emphasising the pedagogical approach to this discipline, rhythmic gymnastics continues to pursue its course as an Olympic sport in full development and in search of media support.

Yet rhythmic gymnastics still holds a shaky place in the world of the sports press. What does it really hold for journalists? Scores, chronometers and records are lacking. Yet photographers and especially reporters, authors of articles in such publications as *Le Monde*, *L'Équipe*, etc., no longer doubt its attraction for the public. The praise continues despite doubts and hesitation. The size of the audience is reasonable and confirms the sport's attraction for the public. Nelson Montfort, a French television journalist, spoke honourably when he said, "The audience likes rhythmic gymnastics!" Where is the attraction? Is it in the strictly feminine side of the sport with its attractive presentation of gymnasts? A seductive body, a pretty face, inspiring elegance? Or is it a composition worthy of the greatest choreographers in modern or classical dance, the continuous game of gravity played out with the apparatus and the risk involved which, in itself, appeals to a sense of creativity and improbability? The answer is most likely a har-

mony of all these aspects. The astonishing subtlety offers the sport a human dimension and thus provides the press and sponsors with a communications tool. Is it not this human dimension that enticed France Telecom to support gymnastics disciplines? The official partner of the French Gymnastics Federation uses gymnastics as a whole, rhythmic gymnastics included, to further its image.

In conclusion, I would state that rhythmic gymnastics has proved to be primarily a sport, then an aesthetic discipline that one either likes or does not like. This choice is completely impossible to control but may be somewhat managed if gymnastics chooses to adapt. Yet let us not forget that rhythmic gymnastics is the queen of passion. He who comes across it runs the risk of never coming away, like a lover it attracts and keeps forever ... is this not enough to fascinate its public?

Rhythmic gymnastics is a physical expression in which femininity and aesthetics are developed through continuous research by performance.   ❖

Former rhythmic gymnast Nadine Blaser, who resides in Paris, is a television commentator and journalist.

*Above: **Greece***
*Opposite: **Evgenia Pavlina (Belarus)***

Opposite: **Three-time world champion Maria Petrova (Bulgaria)**

Clockwise from top left: **Rieko Matsunaga (Japan), Tatiana Ogrizko (Belarus), Tamara Yerofeeva (Ukraine), Mikako Iwamoto (Japan)**

A CELEBRATION

The fans' perspective

A PASSION FOR GYMNASTICS

BY NADINE GIROD

WHEN I was a child I took part in gymnastics classes, and from the start I was fascinated by the best performers in the club. I found it hard not to watch them when they were training or competing. Before long, this interest moved across to televised gymnastics, and eventually I found that I could not miss any event on TV. One of my first memories is of feeling so disappointed for Olga Korbut at the 1973 European Championships in London, when injury prevented her from progressing to the apparatus finals.

Four years later I went to my first international competition—a match between France, Poland, Hungary and Czechoslovakia—and was captivated by the performances of the tiny Vera Cerna, the star of the moment. Thus began my enthusiasm for attending gymnastics events 'live,' and the Junior European Championships in Lyon in 1980 really kept the flame burning for me. However, the most overwhelming memory will doubtless remain my first world championships in Montreal in 1985. I flew there with the French fans—several of whom had already been to Budapest in 1983—and this further stimulated my interest in such a way that I could not wait for the competition to begin.

In Montreal I had a seat in front of the balance beam and was fascinated watching the compulsory exercises, especially the work of the Soviet team. How could they perform with such assurance on a piece of apparatus that had always left me shaking? The team from the USSR achieved an outstanding result with five out of the six girls scoring between 9.90 and 10.0. There is no need to say that this was an exceptional team—Vera Kolesnikova, Irina Baraksanova, Natalia Yurchenko, Elena Shushunova, Oksana Omelianchik and Olga Mostepanova.

After this event I was 'hooked' and knew that from then on I

Opposite: Fan favourite Svetlana Boginskaya (Belarus)

would need to see at least one major gymnastics event each year, a feat I have so far achieved. If only I could be appointed a professional spectator!

There is little comparison between seeing an event 'live' and watching it on TV. On television you can never grasp what is really at stake and the emotion of the event, which when you are there is almost tangible. You do not get a view of the whole event on TV and this can be frustrating. When you sit in an arena you feel a kind of communion with the audience. I have been fortunate to meet and make friends from different countries, and whenever we meet for international championships we acknowledge that we belong to a circle of connoisseurs; we know the competitors, their records, their coaches, their expectations, their disappointments. We appreciate what difficulty there is in the technical elements they perform and we all collect pictures, books, articles and magazines, regretting only that we have no records from the '60s and '70s, having been too young then.

Gymnastics is an art where beauty and emotion merge.

Moreover, when you attend gymnastics competitions something very special happens; you forget all your worries. Nothing else matters, you are beyond time and elated by what you are seeing. Even if you are in low spirits, the thought of a forthcoming event is enough to cheer you up.

For me, gymnastics is an art where beauty and emotion merge. Routines that combine technical performance and artistry just carry me away; there is the realisation that perfection can be part of this world and that magic is at work.

With time, the gymnasts somehow become part of your family. You hope that your favourite ones will succeed and you look forward to seeing their new routines and achievements. You also experience empathy with them; you fall when they fall, you share their moments of triumph, satisfaction and victory. You give the gymnasts the respect they deserve because you know how hard

they work behind the scenes and what courage they need.

Gymnastics can become an obsession and there are times when you even dream of it. Sometimes you feel you have grown up with the gymnasts and thus I followed the career of Svetlana Boginskaya, from her first Junior European title in 1986 to her last European title in 1996, the year she also competed in her third consecutive Olympic Games—a truly impressive achievement. Even when the gymnasts retire your interest in them does not fade, and you would like to know what has become of them and what they feel for the sport at the end of their long careers which began in their childhood.

It is good to know that gymnasts also take strength and encouragement from the support you give them. I clearly remember the 1997 World Championships in Lausanne, when the entire arena erupted into applause for Svetlana Khorkina while she waited for the score on her final piece (asymmetric bars) in the all-around final. When the mark was flashed on the scoreboard the applause turned to cheers and many of us had tears in our eyes.

Watching Svetlana celebrate with her coach, Boris Pilkin, reinforced for me the importance of the relationship between gymnast and coach and how much they rely on each other.

Yet gymnastics is also appealing to those who know nothing about it and this is a measure of its stature as a sport. If the Code of Points appears to be a mystery to them they nonetheless enjoy the spectacle and level of skill on show. A recent development in gymnastics is the Gala or Show event, and the FIG Gala at the Olympic Games in Atlanta—the first of its kind—proved to be a great success and interesting for the spectators since the gymnasts could perform with no pressure. It would seem that this trend will become well established in the future.

Another development seems to be competitions like the World Cup, where gymnasts specialise on their strongest pieces of apparatus. In some ways this could lead to the disappearance of the all-around gymnast who could find it harder to meet the technical requirements, but hopefully the sport will continue to develop in such a way as to support and encourage the specialists as well as the all-around gymnast.

Whichever way the sport develops, gymnastics will remain a passion for someone like me, an anonymous fan. ❖

Nadine Girod is a librarian who resides in France.

Opposite: 1999 world rings champion Dong Zhen, a specialist for China, captivates audiences with his exceptional skills.
Left: Superb grace and expression make Svetlana Khorkina (Russia) popular the world over.

Anna Kovalyova (Russia) received plenty of support from her hometown of Novgorod at the 1998 European Championships in St. Petersburg.

"If I don't win it's still OK. But if I do my
job, then I'm happy."

—*Jordan Jovtchev (Bulgaria)*

Opposite: **Jordan Jovtchev (Bulgaria)**
Above: **Dina Kochetkova (Russia)**

"Most of all, love gymnastics and listen to the coaches,
and everything will happen as it should."

—*Dina Kochetkova (Russia)*

Opposite: **Huang Liping (China)**
Above: **Henrietta Onodi (Hungary)**

Opposite: **Trudy McIntosh (Australia)**
Above: **Blaine Wilson (USA)**

"You train really hard and you've only got one opportunity to make your dream come true."

—*Trudy McIntosh (Australia)*

Opposite: **Lisa Mason (Great Britain)**
Above: **Andrei Kravtsov (Australia)**

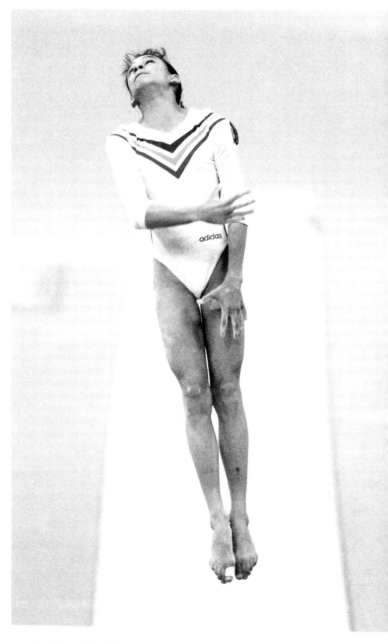

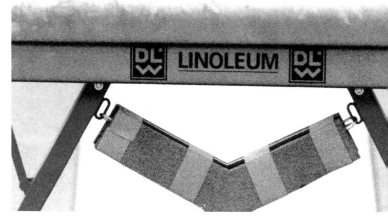

Opposite: Yeo Hong Chul (Korea)
Above: Naoya Tsukahara (Japan)
Right: Andreea Isarescu (Romania)

A New Era

The growth of gymnastics

The various disciplines of the
International Gymnastics
Federation
Clockwise from top left:
Natalia Karpenkova (Belarus)
Russian Women's Pair
Andreea Raducan (Romania)
Evgenia Tchitchiro (Belarus)
Yulia Raskina (Belarus)
Sean Townsend (USA)
Malmö Flickorna (Sweden)

A GLOBAL ACTIVITY

BY HARDY FINK

HUMAN beings have always challenged themselves to explore new dimensions of movement in free space or on and with objects from their environment. They have always done this spontaneously for the sheer joy of it.

Eventually, increased urbanised and sedentary living led to efforts, especially in Europe and China, to formalise movement to improve the fitness of the population. And as always in human society, segments of it developed contests to demonstrate the prowess and superiority of their movement abilities. Those gymnastics contests eventually became included in the first modern Olympic Games and exist within the Olympic movement in more varied and expanded form to this day. It is those evolved structured patterns that have placed gymnastics in the most pivotal centre between art and sport; as the true link between what is important to all humans—movement and aesthetics.

That large range of movement abilities became generally known as physical culture or physical education and was synonymous, for most of the 19th century and the first half of the 20th century, with gymnastics. Thus gymnastics was understood to be all those recreational physical activities performed in free space, on apparatus of various design and with hand-held apparatus of various types. Though the general public has strayed from that understanding of gymnastics, the reality of it as the foundation for a fit human being prepared to tackle any other physical challenge has not changed one bit.

The truth of that statement is more evident now than ever before. At least 20 million children around the world participate in structured gymnastics programmes; the overwhelming majority because they love new movement experiences, they love physical challenge, they love the advantage it gives them in any other activity over their non-gymnastics peers. These things bring real joy and they constitute what is the glory of gymnastics. And for those very few for whom it is the right thing, there is opportunity to explore and expand the boundaries of human movement capability in all levels of competition up to the Olympic Games.

The International Gymnastics Federation (FIG) has, in recent decades, made a number of decisions to expand the variety of gymnastics experience, to bring it back to being synonymous

with physical education.

The general gymnastics experience is most magnificently presented in the Gymnaestrada, which most recently attracted over 20,000 participants eager to demonstrate their abilities in a non-competitive setting of pure joy of movement. This magnificent festival of music, pageantry and movement reflects the core of the gymnastics experience. Rhythmic gymnastics was included in the 1960s and adds an important dimension of grace and unbelievable hand-eye coordination.

Three other activities have more recently been added to the repertoire of FIG sports, and these will enormously expand the richness of the human movement—the gymnastics—experience. Trampoline provides the general public with a more accessible experience of spatial orientation and the opportunity for the few of expanding the limits of human spatial awareness. Sports aerobics—aerobic gymnastics in my terminology—merges the basics of physical fitness with gymnastics patterns for an exciting and very accessible new sporting experience. Finally, sports acrobatics—acrobatic gymnastics—allows the exploration and expression of free space gymnastics patterns in cooperation with one or more partners.

Together, the gymnastics experience has enriched a large series of traditional sports and even spawned some new ones, the "adrenaline" or "extreme" sports most prominent among them. One need only mention diving, aerial skiing, trick sky diving, break dancing, skate boarding, BMX biking, rock climbing, equestrian vaulting, circus activities, combative sports, etc., to realise that without a strong grounding in gymnastics, most

*Opposite top: **Mario Americo of Brazil (sports aerobics)***
*Opposite bottom: **Holland (general gymnastics)***

165

would be diminished and some could not exist.

The future of gymnastics is guaranteed because, I believe, it will again come to mean physical education. Once again we are facing the prospect of an ever more sedentary and less fit world-wide population. At the same time the public is increasingly enchanted by the media presentation of those exploring the human movement experience. I predict that these factors will bring increasing numbers to participate in gymnastics, to use gymnastics for improved fitness, or to use gymnastics in preparation for other activities.

The expanded competitive gymnastics options—Gymnaestrada, artistic, rhythmic, trampoline, aerobic, acrobatic—will also permit gymnasts to participate for longer and with more personal success experiences. In what many still consider the traditional gymnastics sport—artistic gymnastics—the FIG has also recently permitted gymnasts to compete on only one or several apparatus. This has already allowed competitive gymnasts to stay active longer without the demands of continually preparing for many apparatus. The FIG has also worked actively to pro-

Gymnastics is a lifetime activity that enhances the quality of life for all those who participate.

vide and to nurture the gymnastics experience in all 122 member countries.

It is now our collective task to present gymnastics in a manner that permits the public and media and politicians to understand what it is. It is not a series of dangerous stunts. It is not the competitive sport shown on television. It is the human movement experience. It is the link between art and sport. It is a lifetime activity that enhances the quality of life for all those who participate. It brings joy and fitness and challenge. We have sold our wonderful activity short by allowing or perpetuating the focus to be primarily on the Olympic athlete. That is also a part of gymnastics and it is the right part for some gymnasts. But it is a minuscule part of the enormous whole, and it has been permitted to hide the importance of gymnastics to society. It is up to us to bring the truth back to public attention. The FIG's recent decisions are on the right path to do just that. ❖

Hardy Fink of Canada is the Men's Technical Committee President of the Fédération Internationale de Gymnastique.

*Opposite: **Tamara Yerofeeva** of Ukraine (rhythmic gymnastics)*
*Right: **Vanessa Atler** of the U.S. (women's artistic gymnastics)*

"Improvement is reflected in and measured by the continued increase in difficulty of performances. Without such continuous improvement and progress, the sport would soon stagnate."

—*Hardy Fink (Canada)*

A SPORT FOR ANYONE

BY MARGARET SIKKENS AHLQUIST

ONE of the most wonderful things about gymnastics is that it can be practised by anyone, no matter what age, size, sex or skill level. This has always been the case and I am sure it will be even more evident in the coming years. General gymnastics is the important base for all sports, and everyone should be able to enjoy the happiness that comes from taking part.

When I am asked to define general gymnastics it gives me the opportunity to reflect on its nature. Within the FIG we use a definition which can be used all over the world, and for that reason it is quite a wide one and everyone who works within it will have their own picture of it. For me the big value is the happiness you experience together with your gymnasts. That can be meeting people, the creation of something together and travelling to other cities and countries for performances. It can also be that great

> *General gymnastics is the important base for all sports, and everyone should be able to enjoy the happiness that comes from taking part.*

feeling you get when you perform that perfect movement together with the rest of the gymnasts in the group, the smiles on faces and the laughter together.

General gymnastics can be a small child hanging upside-down from the bar laughing for joy and the next minute skipping around the gym to cheerful music. It can also be the over-sized gentleman working hard during his aerobic lesson. In another place it is a youth group working on its new performance programme. It can also be a gymnastics-dance performed at a high level and with difficult skills. One hour later it could be a mixed group of boys and girls practising tumbling and vaulting—they are quite young and inexperienced so they are working hard at the basics of gymnastics. To achieve quality at any level it is necessary to work correctly from the beginning! So as you see, there is no easy answer to the question of what general gymnastics is but as you understand it is for everyone and it is fun. No limits!

The FIG is unique in many ways but I am especially glad for the way this international sports federation is giving so much importance to the very base of its sport. With its own committee for general gymnastics, the FIG is giving the opportunity for gymnasts from all over the world to be members of this great world sports family. The committee promotes and stimulates general gymnastics through its main event, the Gymnaestrada.

We always hope that our competitive gymnasts who are at the

*Opposite: **Malmö Flickorna of Sweden***
*Left: **South Africa***

top level of the sport will want to stay in gymnastics when they come to the end of their careers, and offering them the chance to take part in general gymnastics is important and necessary but it does not mean they have to take part in low quality and unchallenging activities. It is actually the other way around. Of course, we have to find alternatives for them when they stop and we know how difficult it is to be on the top level for such a short time and therefore general gymnastics has to be the natural base to which they can return.

There is a place where gymnasts from all five continents can meet and experience the biggest gymnastics happening there is and this place is the World Gymnaestrada. Every fourth year gymnasts from the entire world gather together for this wonderful event. Throughout the week coaches and gymnasts can see and experience what general gymnastics can be and they can find

---

Every fourth year gymnasts from the entire world gather together for this wonderful event (World Gymnaestrada).

new inspiration for their future work. A Gymnaestrada is a big event and the pleasure, joy, happiness and laughter lasts a lifetime. In 1999 more than 22,000 gymnasts came together in Gothenburg, Sweden, and hopefully even more member federations will find their way to future events.

The future of general gymnastics will be decided by the gymnasts themselves. It is developing all the time and the federation needs to monitor this development, nurture it and spread it further. We hope to attract more people who participate in gymnastics. One of the good things about general gymnastics is that it is easy. We don't need expensive apparatus or complicated buildings to get going. The fantasy and power of invention mixed with knowledge and the interest of getting people in motion is the answer.

So I will end as I started. One of the most wonderful things about gymnastics is that it can be practised by anyone, no matter what age, size, sex or skill level. Gymnastics is for everyone. Enjoy it!   ❖

Margaret Sikkens Ahlquist of Sweden is a physical education teacher with 27 years' experience as a gymnastics instructor. She is the General Gymnastics Committee President of the Fédération Internationale de Gymnastique and instructs many international courses. She has been with the FIG authority since 1992 and has worked at the Swedish Gymnastics Federation and at Lillsved Gymnastics College.

Switzerland

Opposite: **Italy**
Above: **Germany**

"Gymnastics is universal. It is educational, sportive and it is, in some way, life, with its shadows and lights. It is equally an example, a life model for all."

—Bruno Grandi (FIG President, Italy)

Left: Sweden, arm in arm
Above: Germany

CHALLENGING GRAVITY

BY JOHN BEETON

THE sport of trampolining is as old as man, a reflection of his desire to defy the ever-pervading presence of gravity.

Several cultures have devised apparatus to send an athlete into the air, such as an outstretched animal skin to throw up and safely receive the descending performer. Circuses have used a number of devices to show off aerial and floor somersault activity.

The way the sport is now practised reflects the intrusion, delightful in this instance, of modern technology. Trampolining has only emerged in the last 49 to 50 years from the 1936 prototype apparatus built in an Iowa garage by Larry Griswold and one

> *The way the activity is now practised reflects the instrusion, delightful in this instance, of modern technology.*

of his tumbling students, George Nissen.

The Air Force and later the Space Agencies were not slow to employ trampolines with their pilots and astronauts. Medical authorities and those working with handicapped persons have found many exciting benefits from trampoline use. At the recreational level trampolining has an immediate appeal, especially for young people.

Every era produces at least one step forward in the sophistication of a trampoline machine. The most modern ones are capable of projecting an athlete to such a height that the top stars can touch 10 metre-high ceilings and perform repetition triple somersaults with ease.

Competitive activity commenced in the U.S. at the conclusion of World War ll, developing and growing as a sport in colleges. The activity spread to Europe in the 1950s, inspired by visits from Nissen, and display teams took the activity to all continents

Opposite: **Ryan Weston** *(USA)*

Above: **Daisuke Nakata** *(Japan)*

In 1964 the International Trampoline Federation was formed with seven founder federations.

in the late 1950s and early 1960s, when many national federations were formed. In 1958 the first Nissen Cup was held in Switzerland, under the organisation of Kurt Bachler, another pioneer of the sport, and it is an event which still continues today.

In 1964 the International Trampoline Federation (FIT) was formed with seven founder member federations. Championship activity continued to develop and has grown continuously year by year. Annual world championships were held from 1964, though since 1968 they have been held every other year, with European championships started in 1969 and Pan American championships in 1981. In addition, European Youth championships have been held every other year since 1972, and the introduction of the World Cup event in 1993 has seen a tremendous growth, with television companies giving live coverage to most events throughout the series. Trampolining has been a World Games sport since 1981 and the World Age Group Games always attracts a large entry—between 1,000 to 1,200 athletes!

In the early days, U.S. athletes took many titles, though a number of nations have since shared in the top honours, especially athletes from the former Soviet Union. This breathtaking sport is now well known across the world and gymnasts are able to execute astonishing somersaults at great height with a multitude of complex twists and turns. As well as being a sport in its own right, it is widely recognised as a training tool for many other sports such as gymnastics, diving, freestyle skiing and so on. In 1998, at the first-ever Olympic Gymnastics Gala in Atlanta, trampolining was performed and the following year its application for Olympic status was granted by the International Olympic Committee. This necessitated merging with the International Gymnastics Federation (FIG), a complex and challenging business that was successfully accomplished at the end of 1998. Thus, for the first time, trampolining will take part at the 2000 Olympic Games in Sydney.

As a member sporting discipline of the FIG, trampoline sports

Left: Alexander Russakov (Russia)
Opposite left: Robyn Forbes (Australia)
Opposite right: Jennifer Parilla (USA)

"I love the fear. I love the heights.

I love extreme sports."

—*Jennifer Parilla (USA)*

will widen the choice of the gymnastic family whilst at the same time provide a new market for the media and spectators alike. There will be the possibility for spectacular shows in combination with the other gymnastic disciplines. There will also be a new vision for gymnastics where female gymnasts can be seen to be participating as mature women able to compete at the highest level. The sport will also bring many technical experts to the gymnastics family, especially in the field of biomechanics, and sponsors will have the opportunity to 'brand' a completely new discipline that is full of movement, grace and strength.

The 'marriage' of trampoline and other gymnastic disciplines has been long overdue and this coming together offers an even more dynamic and stronger FIG.   ❖

John Beeton is from Scotland and is a member of the Trampolining Commission of the Fédération Internationale de Gymnastique.

*Opposite: **Alan Villafuerte (Holland)***
*Above: **Aurore Monin (France)***
*Right: **German Khnytchev (Russia)***

Opposite: **Irina Karavaeva (Russia)**
Above: **Lenka Honzakova and Petra**
Vachnokova (Czech Republic)

Diep Tuan Cuong (Vietnam)

A FITNESS EVOLUTION

BY HOLLY ABRAHAM

SPORTS aerobics is constantly evolving. Many of us at the international level feel rather overawed being part of a 100-year-old organisation such as the FIG. Its history, credibility and influence in the world of sport require us to speed ahead in our own development. Many participants are inexperienced at international level and find the challenge of meeting the expectations of the FIG quite daunting. Many countries are struggling with partnerships between aerobics and gymnastics that no other discipline in the FIG has had to develop.

We want to create an identity for the sport that is different from artistic or rhythmic gymnastics, yet at the same time we need to have some similarity in order to be accepted. We are the sport with funny hair, wild costumes and loud music. I feel we are following *and* creating a trend. The huge fitness movement that is our foundation continually changes. Young people all over the globe are flocking to fitness facilities where programmes are constantly evolving with the latest trends. There is aerobics with boxing, aerobics with martial arts movements and the use of different apparatus in a class designed to entertain as well as tone. All it will take is for some entrepreneurs to introduce gymnastic elements into the aerobics class and we will then have another trend in the fitness community.

Sports aerobics capitalises on a trend that has been 20 years in the making. The fitness philosophy is based on music that is fun and entertaining, participants keeping time with the music and being synchronised within the group. We want to keep the philosophy of aerobics while developing a high performance sport for gymnastics. It offers a new discipline to those athletes who have retired from gymnastics and who already have excellent mental and physical preparation. Gymnasts who compete for the first time in sports aerobics have a style that they have brought from artistic or rhythmic gymnastics. The ballet technique is evidence of past experiences as an athlete. Many athletes at the 1999 Hannover World Championships showed significant changes in

> *The huge fitness movement that is our foundation continually changes.*

style and had adopted a more defined, precise aerobic technique that demonstrated the learning process that athletes must go through. Sports aerobics has modernised a traditional sport discipline in much the same way as beach volleyball has developed a new facet of volleyball.

The evaluation of the current Code of Points enables the Sports Aerobics Commission to realise how athletes and coaches think, how they interpret information and how the Code should change in order to direct the sport. Open difficulty is a key concept of all FIG disciplines. The athletes in each FIG discipline have a history of virtuosity, risk and reward for going beyond what the authors of the Code have envisioned. Sports aerobics must continue along this path.

The routines can be developed further with a balance between high performance athletic skills and interpretation of the music, humour, emotion and artistry of the athletes. Competitors that have incredible rhythm, style and power combined with a high degree of difficulty are cheered with the greatest effort by the spectators.

My ultimate goal is to be part of the group that brings sports aerobics to the Olympic Games. As part of the team that is creating a Code of Points, I hope to help the development in each country. ❖

As president of Sports Leadership Group, Holly Abraham organises national and provincial sports aerobics competitions and special events in conjunction with the fitness industry. She is an international presenter and a course conductor for the National Coaching Certification programme in Canada. She is currently a member of the Sports Aerobics Technical Commission of the Fédération Internationale de Gymnastique.

Opposite: **Constanza Popova, Kalojan Kolovanov (Bulgaria)**

Above: **Beata Storczer, Ferenc Szegedi (Hungary)**

Opposite: Yuriko Ito (Japan)
Right: 1998 Aerobics World Championships Opening Ceremonies
Below: French Men's Trio

AN ANCIENT SPORT

BY YURI STEPCHENKOV

SPORTS acrobatics is one of the oldest disciplines in the world of sport and it has seen many stages in its development. It became a professional sport maybe 300 or more years ago with street entertainers and theatre performers. In fact, the first double back somersault was performed in 1902 in the Russian circus.

In 1973 the International Federation of Sports Acrobatics (IFSA) was formed and the first world championships were held in 1974 in Moscow. This was a great success and the competitive sport developed rapidly after this. Many of the champions from this event have become coaches of our current stars. Seven disciplines were established, including tumbling. During the life of IFSA, 15 world championships were held plus many European championships and World Cup events. More than 50 countries became member federations making it a truly global sport.

All over the world new unions and relationships are being forged—politically and in the world of sport—and by becoming part of the FIG family, sports acrobatics is mirroring this trend and will gain more exposure. Whilst some may feel that we have 'lost' two of our disciplines (men's and women's tumbling which are now part of the world trampoline championships), there is no doubt that we have gained much more and the future is full of challenges, new horizons and new discoveries.

The unique feature of our sport is that unlike the other competitive disciplines in the FIG, sports acrobatics is suitable for all types of physiques, from the small gymnast who is on the top to the bigger and stronger ones who support. This diversity also means that as young gymnasts grow, they can change positions and still stay in the sport. This is important to age group programmes and junior development. In some countries (notably Russia and Bulgaria) we even have family development programmes, where routines are done together. It is one of the few sports which enables families to spend more time together and develop communication between them.

Being a contact sport, sports acrobatics develops physical skills of balance and control but also real trust and reliance. Gymnasts

Sports acrobatics is suitable for all types of physiques, ...

who compete together in this way invariably become friends for life. It develops psychological strength, patience and tolerance to your partner and all the others around you. Leadership qualities are developed and these are not necessarily always in the supporting gymnast. Sports acrobatics aids aerobic and anaerobic fitness and there's no doubt that it is a demanding and challenging sport.

Having been a competitor at the highest level has given me great insight into the sport and a real understanding of what it needs. My competitive career was a challenging time and with my partner, Gennadi Terischenko, I had to work hard to fight my way to the top of the Soviet system. At any time, as many as 11 men's pairs were at the same level battling to become national champions and thus win the right to compete for a world title. There was a great deal of pressure but I gained immeasurably from the sport and it opened up the world for me.

It has been a natural progression for me to become an official and my experience as a competitor has been a big advantage. I have many hopes and ambitions for sports acrobatics and would like to see it develop through more TV coverage; if it becomes more easily understood by the audience, more attractive to spectators, then everyone will feel that they can do it and want to get involved. We need to reconsider the Code of Points, not only in terms of difficulty, but develop it so that it encourages the harmonious development of the participant and helps to contribute positively to society.

The name sports acrobatics comes from the Latin meaning "climbing up" and our sport always tried to progress and move upward. As new members of the FIG we are confident that we will continue to do so. ❖

Yuri Stepchenkov is President of the Sports Acrobatics Commission of the Fédération Internationale de Gymnastique. With his partner, Gennadi Terischenko, he became world champion in Men's Pairs and won several European and World Cup titles.

Opposite: U.S. Women's Pair

Above: **Women's Pair from the former Soviet Union**

Opposite: **Chinese Men's Group**

Opposite: **Ukrainian Men's Pair**
Below: **Belgian Mixed Pair**
Right: **Ukrainian Women's Trio**

"The partnering nature of acro teaches
individuals to cooperate with one another."

—*George Nissen (USA)*

GYMNASTS WERE HERE

THE EVENT IS over, the arena falls silent, the cheers and applause fade away. For some the competition brought satisfaction, the fulfilment of their ambitions and reward for their efforts. For others, a sense of disappointment and the determination to do better next time.

The efforts of the gymnasts leave memories which can only be expressed in superlatives. Their performances recorded in words and on film for posterity are also etched into the memories of the spectators.

The chalk dust settles and leaves tangible impressions of what has taken place. The gymnasts leave their imprints which for a short time longer preserve and bear testimony to what has gone before.

Gymnasts were here.   —*Eileen Langsley*

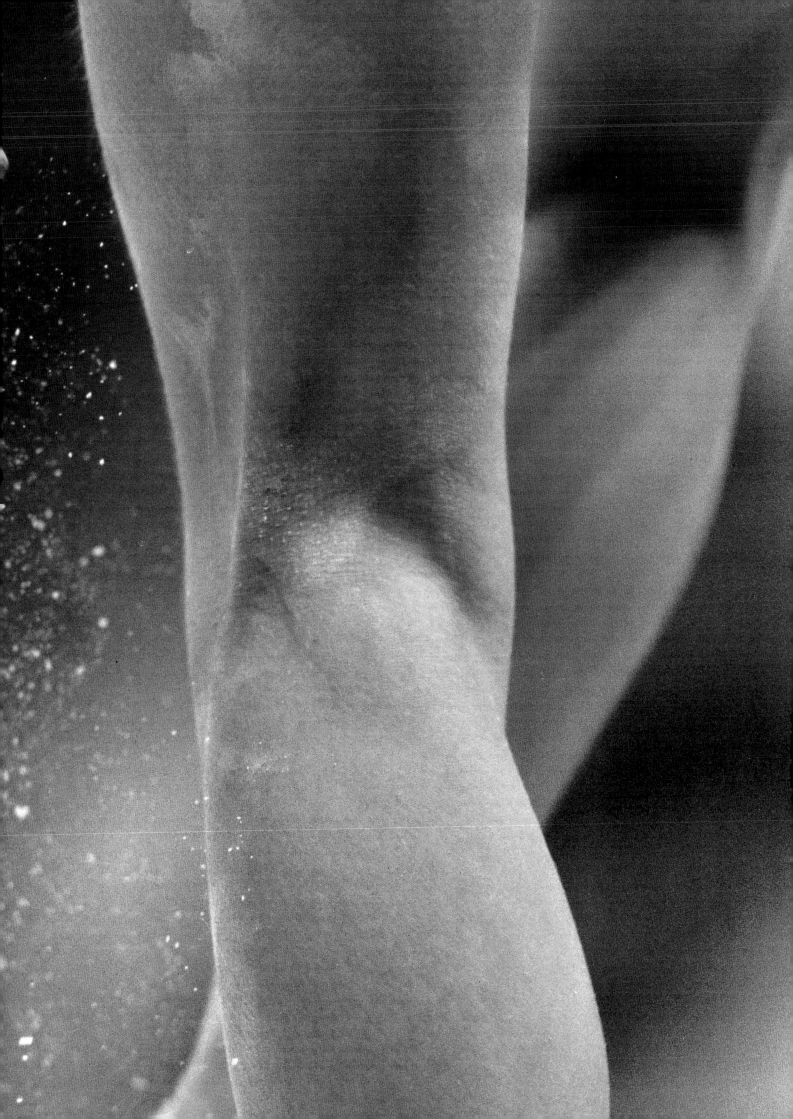

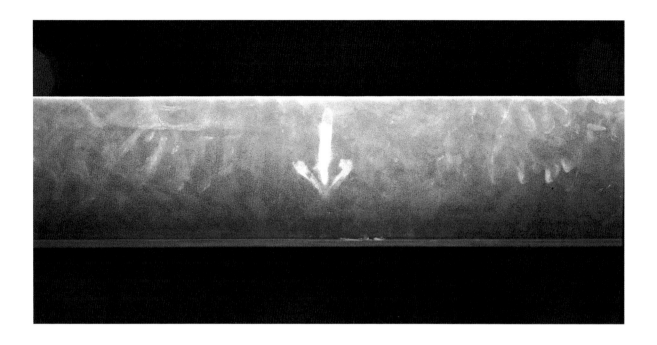

"We must remember that ultimately we are our own judges and find the inner satisfaction that comes from honest self appraisal and knowing that you've done your best."

—*Toby Towson (USA)*

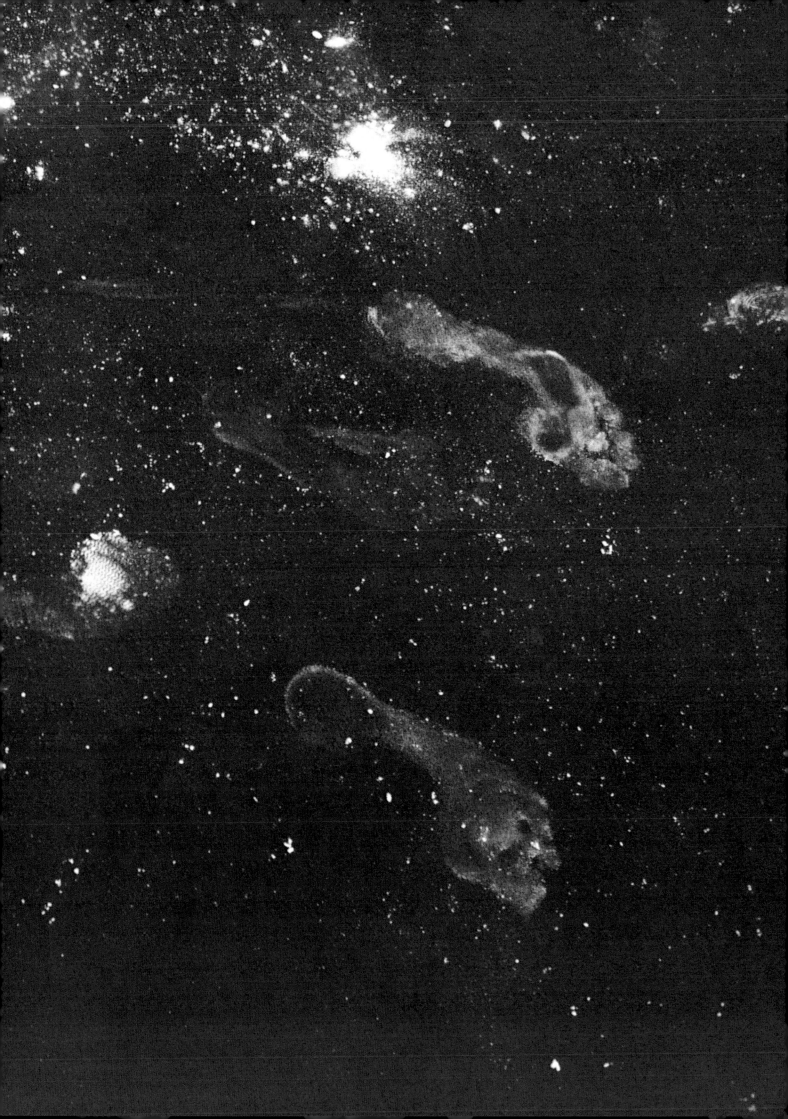

"When I look back on my gymnastics career and life, I feel very happy. My only wish is that people around the world could live in peace and happiness and fight only on the fields of sport!"

—*Leon Stukelj (Slovenia)*

ACKNOWLEDGEMENTS

Once again, the FIG would like to acknowledge the support of LONGINES, not only for their sponsorship of this publication but for all their work and expertise which have ensured the smooth running of FIG events in recent years.

Thanks and recognition go to FIG President Bruno Grandi and all the members of the FIG Executive Committee for their vision and wholehearted support of this project, and also to Slava Corn, President of the FIG Media Commission.

Special thanks go to Paul Ziert, publisher of *International Gymnast* magazine, for willingly providing the technical facilities which were extensively used for the design stages of the book, and also for his kind permission to reproduce quotes from articles and interviews in IG in recent years.

Also giving permission for quotes to be used from their magazines were André Gueisbuhler of *World of Gymnastics* magazine (published by the FIG), Sarah Baldwin of *Gym Stars* magazine, Trevor Low of *The Gymnast* magazine and Katy Vilarino of *L'Hebdo*.

Gratitude is expressed to all at ROOS SA for their technical excellence and expertise in the production of the book.

Thanks to Redheads Colour Laboratories (Sheffield, Great Britain) and especially to Frank Jeffcock for quality colour prints.

Thanks to AJ. Stephenson for assistance with technical support and services.

Gratitude is expressed to the following who helped with interpretation, translation and liaison: Gary Alexander, Vera and John Atkinson, Michel Boutard, Norbert Bueche, Silvia Cigoli, Warwick Forbes, Yuko Grivel, Susi Guenther Kroeger, Gao Jin, Yoshiko Kamo, Pavel Kotov, Zhong Ling, Herbert Lorenz, Maria Marcassa, Yolande Perroulaz, Becky Riti, Sandra Stadelmann, Adrian Stan, Valentin Stoica, Iwona Szychowska, Irina Viner, Gary Warren, Tamara Yatchenko.

Finally, my deepest appreciation to all those gymnasts, coaches and officials, members of the media and fans who have contributed their thoughts in writing for this book, and as ever my gratitude to Dwight Normile for his work and support and my admiration for his vision and artistry.

The book is dedicated to all the gymnasts and coaches who have inspired and challenged me in more than 20 years of photographing gymnastics.

—*Eileen Langsley*